SHORT ORDER DAD

SHORT ORDER DAD

One Guy's Guide to Making Food Fun and Hassle-Free

BY ROBERT ROSENTHAL

Skyhorse Publishing

Library of Congress Cataloging-in-Publication Data is available on file.

All interior photos by Josephine Rozman, except where noted.

Cover design by Jane Sheppard
Cover photo credit iStockphoto (top) and Josephine Rozman (bottom)

ISBN: 978-1-63450-980-0
Ebook ISBN: 978-1-63450-981-7

Printed in China

To Carolyn, Ariana, and Veronica,
who make every meal together special.

"Rob Rosenthal's approach to the kitchen is commonsensical, whimsical, and above all intelligible—which is by no means always the case in cookbooks these days. He obviously loves preparing good food as much as he loves eating it, and he knows how to convey his affection with those two admirable writerly virtues: clarity and wit. This book will have you cooking, and probably smiling, in, er, short order."

—Colman Andrews, editorial director, *The Daily Meal*; eight-time James Beard award–winning author

"When was the last time you smiled your way through an entire cookbook? Every single recipe in Rob Rosenthal's *Short Order Dad* is one you want to (and actually can) cook. While incredibly informative and a great handbook for novices and seasoned cooks alike, this book gives you the sense that above all, cooking is about relaxing, creating pleasure, and having fun."

—Danny Meyer, restaurateur and author, *Setting the Table*

"I'm convinced that if we all had a dad like Rob Rosenthal, the world would be a happier, healthier place. His command of the stove, and ability to distill even the most complicated cooking techniques into applicable, intuitive recipes and advice, proves that a man's place is most certainly in the kitchen. *Short Order Dad* is delicious fun for the whole family! It's such a great book—I can't wait to get it for my own dad, brothers, husband, best friend, uncle, and nephew."

—Gail Simmons, food expert and author of *Talking with My Mouth Full*

"This book breaks it down; it's in Robert's voice too, which cracks me up. It has the power to make the most mannish dad novices earn the confidence in the kitchen to please crowds. I even got some ideas for the menu at Little Owl."

—Joey Campanaro, chef and owner, Little Owl (Greenwich Village, NYC)

"*Short Order Dad* is a simple, fun book that encompasses all the aspects of a good home cookbook; his philosophies of never wasting a meal, or his connection to food through his family and heritage, is the way everyone should cook and eat. Robert's love for food and cooking is evident in the way the book is laid out. His approach to all aspects of cooking a meal, from tools to techniques to shopping, is a great layperson's guide to everyday cooking. His recipes are well chosen and not fussy or complicated. If you know Robert, the only thing missing while you cook from this book is his physical presence; his voice and joyful character are embodied in every word of the book."

—Floyd Cardoz, chef, Paowalla (NYC) and The Bombay Canteen (India); winner, *Top Chef Masters*

"I've personally tasted some of Rob's delicious cooking at parties that he's thrown and I'm super psyched to see him put all of his recipes into this book. Now dads across America can join in the fun, thanks to Rob."

—Bill Telepan, chef, Telepan Restaurant; executive chef, Wellness in the Schools

"Listen up, men! *Nothing* is sexier than a guy who can cook for his family, and Chef Rosenthal delivers the power tools necessary to gain confidence in the kitchen. This hilarious manual provides the road map that every savvy man needs to turn his kitchen into a culinary playground."

—David and Veronica James, authors of *Going Gypsy: One Couple's Adventure from Empty Nest to No Nest at All*

TABLE OF CONTENTS

"You should have fun in the kitchen and then emerge from it with flavorful, wholesome, attractive dishes that can be served to both family and guests."
—Jacques Pépin (French chef, TV personality, author)

ACKNOWLEDGMENTS

I have a lot to be grateful for, since I was fortunate to be born in the right place at the right time to the right people. Believe me when I tell you that when your father is a lawyer and your mother is a guidance counselor, you'll never be short on advice, direction, or understanding. Yet it was their unconditional love that meant and taught me the most.

Writing a book, it turns out, is not possible without the support and encouragement of friends, advisors, and professionals. Among the people I have to thank for their various contributions and assorted assistance along the way are Ann Wijkström, Richard Lewis, Missy Chase Lapine, Victoria Rowan, Kenny Pena, and Linda "Gemma" Thomas. Plus a shout-out as well to my agent, Sharon Bowers, and editor, Julie Ganz, for their work in bringing this book to fruition.

Three people merit extra special mention. Josephine Rozman is my gifted photographer who took all of the food photos you see within. Not only a pleasure to work with, her aesthetic was invaluable in making my food look as good and appealing as it can. Mitchell Goldman, from the very beginning, has been instrumental in helping and supporting me in every possible way, as a producer, muse, enforcer, and friend. And my brother Laurence, whose many talents and profound wisdom have always been and continue to be indispensable to me.

My deepest love and endless appreciation goes to the three loves in my life, whom I passionately adore—Carolyn, Ariana, and Veronica— who inspire me and bring me happiness every single day.

RR

INTRODUCTION

Whoever originated the phrase "don't play with your food" had it all wrong. I actually think of the kitchen as a place to play.

Long before I graduated from cooking school, I was a busy advertising executive, moonlighting as a standup comedian, with a working wife and two daughters. I was also the designated cook, balancing the schedules of an active family as well as entertaining our friends. That's when my girls named me "Short Order Dad." Over the years my method was honed to feed my family and friends, and for us all to have a good time while doing it.

Learning the art of the punch line is more valuable than just getting laughs; it teaches you to edit down to the essentials. In *Short Order Dad*, I'm sharing the simple techniques I've collected over the years, a basic toolkit, and a solid playbook of 100 recipes that will help you achieve *the most taste with the fewest ingredients and the least effort*™. This is not just family meals either, nor is it all necessarily kid-friendly. Rather, it's about preparing delicious food that will satisfy the most discerning folks out there, whatever the occasion may be.

My mission now is to share the joy of making great-tasting meals—and bring the fun to food. You'll find that even though I have a fancy cooking degree, I'm not a fancy guy. I went to cooking school, but you don't have to. I can tell you what you need to know to make you a meal master in the minimum time.

Good cooking doesn't have to be complicated to be great. In fact, it's just the opposite. So whether you're clueless in the kitchen, pan-fry phobic, or already a skilled cook, *Short Order Dad* is here to help. All you have to remember is this: Life is short. *Never waste a meal*™.

CHAPTER ONE

NEVER WASTE A MEAL™

The evolution of my essential philosophy

Gentlemen, I know what it's like to be a guy. I've been one my whole life. I like it. And I have no plans to "transition." What distinguishes me from most men, however—men who think nothing of having fast-food fries and a chocolate shake for lunch—is that I am a total "foodie." That means I spend an awful lot of my time focused on food, always thinking about my next meal, even as I'm consuming the current one. I'm interested in any type of food, from anywhere, whether it's a food truck or a fancy joint, as long as it's great to eat.

The second point that separates me from others is that I have had a love affair with food ever since I was breast-fed. I believe it started then. Fresh, local, organic—rules I still try to live by.

Most kids I know were satisfied by a can of SpaghettiOs for lunch. Not me. My palate started becoming refined very early on. I really noticed tastes.

Okay, you might say, most guys like to eat. Yet how many guys do you know who regularly do the cooking? A lot of guys would think of this as a burden. For others, like me, it's a pleasure. I'm happy to say, though, that change is in the air. More than ever before, guys are handling the cooking in the household. It's like the 100th Monkey Syndrome. (Not that men are like monkeys, but a recent *New York Times* article was actually headlined, "Chimpanzees Would Cook if Given the Chance, Research Says.") No, this phenomenon refers to a sudden leap or tipping point that occurs when a critical mass of people (or animals) begin doing something new. Everyone in vastly different locations begin to change behavior. And that seems to be what's happening with men in the kitchen. All over the country, more guys are actually finding it interesting and pleasurable to cook.

In fact, all the significant memories of my life are connected to food. Most people vividly recall their first sexual experience with rapturous nostalgia. Me? I'll never forget my first . . . piece of pizza, which, incidentally, was not unlike my first sexual experience—very hot and over too soon.

Life is short. Never waste a meal.

Given the circumstances of my upbringing, I'm not entirely sure how my passion was ignited. They say your connection to food starts with your family, but mine must have skipped a generation. Neither of my parents was particularly adept in the kitchen. My father was a lawyer and an outstanding man. Unfortunately, he had no discernible taste buds; he'd be happy eating dog food if it was served with sautéed onions on it. My mother is a force of nature with a master's degree, and was a busy high school guidance counselor for thirty years, but when it came to her culinary skills, let's just say that no one baked a better potato. I enjoyed her pre-packaged TV dinners (particularly the fried chicken) and her other specialty, Mrs. Paul's frozen fish sticks with a side of spaghetti that she covered with her "tomato sauce" made of ketchup and butter. (It was good, by the way.)

My grandparents, on the other hand, were deeply connected to food, and they must be where I got the bug. My grandfather was a Russian immigrant. One of the reasons I loved him was because he had a great sense of humor. And he fed me. You see, he owned his own butcher shop, and every Thursday after work he would come to our apartment bearing gifts: a big box of assorted meats,

including chicken, steak, lamb chops, and liver. The first thing my mother did when he arrived was to open the prize package of "chop meat," which was wrapped in brown butcher paper. Then we each scooped up two fingers worth of this raw beef, topped it with a sprinkle of salt, and eagerly swallowed it down. At two years old, I had no idea I was basically eating steak tartare, but I knew I liked its smooth, rich, deep primal flavor—the essence of beef. To this day, I consider steak tartare and a gin martini my "happy meal."

As a kid, it was exciting for me to go to my grandparents' apartment because my grandmother was always in the kitchen cooking and the smells were intoxicating. She was an amazing cook who made an unforgettable vegetable soup, stuffed cabbage, potato pancakes, and gingerbread men (with Red Hots for eyes and raisins for a smile). I took equal delight in any food they had sitting around, like the bowl of Wise potato chips or the Chunky chocolate candy bars on the cocktail table in the living room. I loved the combined tastes of the crispy, salty chips and the creamy, sweet milk chocolate

loaded with crunchy peanuts and chewy raisins. They were ideal together, and it was my first experience with "complementary" tastes—that coalescence of sweet and salty that makes your taste buds sing like a soprano.

In my family, every occasion revolved around food. This included, but was not limited to, birth and death. Although I wasn't entirely conscious at my own circumcision, there are two things I'm sure of. One is that it hurt like hell. The other is that they served whitefish salad. That's just what my people do—clip the tip off a baby's most sensitive body part, and then give everyone else some smoked fish in celebration. Frankly, given the way I was introduced to this particular delicacy, my fondness for whitefish salad surprises me to this day. (You'd think my unconscious mind would send me running the opposite way.) Yet even now, I consider a creamy, slightly smoky whitefish salad on a fresh, chewy New York bagel to be perhaps the best sandwich in the world.

I actually remember every meal I've had—the good, of course, but even the bad. In fact, the whole timeline of my life can be expressed through the foods I ate at every stage. It changed, naturally, as the sophistication of my palate changed. In camp, there was my first peanut butter and jelly sandwich. In the Puerto Rican rain forest on our very first family vacation, we had these amazing fried shrimp in the rain forest. Growing up, I always looked forward to the eggs over easy with toast and hash browns at the local coffee shop. In junior high school, it was those fat, rippled French fries at Nathan's and the enormous chocolate chunks in the ice cream we had at a local place called Itgen's. As a teen, I'll never forget the absolute exhilaration I experienced the first time I tried a sausage and pepper hero at a street fair. The spaghetti with meat sauce and meatball heroes from the lunch ladies in high school made Wednesdays a particularly special day of the week. Then, of course, there's the homemade falafel and tahini that my friend Alan's mom made us in tenth grade, followed by the disgust that always registered on our physics teacher's face when we came to seventh period reeking of garlic.

Even my boyhood idols were connected to food. It's not that I didn't admire great baseball players, movie stars, and world leaders, like everyone else. But unlike other boys, there was no one I followed more closely than a guy named Graham Kerr, otherwise known as the "Galloping Gourmet." I admit this wasn't common behavior, like watching *Charlie's Angels* or *CHiPs*. There I was, ten years old and watching his daily TV program where he would whip up an elaborate and scrumptious French meal in front of a live audience. I think what drew me to it the most was that he had such a blast doing it (perhaps aided by the entire bottle of wine he managed to polish off before each half-hour show was finished). Every episode would end with Kerr inviting someone from the audience to share this marvelous meal he had just constructed with tremendous humor and panache. And each time, he wore that same sublime expression of pleasure on his face as he tasted his own masterpiece. His was a response of such supreme, otherworldly satisfaction.

Who wouldn't want to learn to cook after that? He made it seem so alluring. So of course the desire to feel that way started to grow in me, and sooner or later, the tree was bound to bear fruit. For my parents' anniversary, I decided to surprise them and replicate one of his meals. It was called *crêpe des fruits de la mer*, more commonly referred to as seafood crepes. I served it with a fresh, clean cucumber salad. My parents recall it being delicious, but I'm afraid the white wine sauce was way too sophisticated for my immature palate.

My parents divorced when I was thirteen. I realize that divorce is painful for most kids, but for me, it actually worked out pretty well, in one way at least. The divorce prompted my father to move to Manhattan, and my brother and I got to spend every weekend there with him. As I said, my parents were part of the generation that wasn't interested in cooking, so naturally the man never once used the kitchen in his apartment, which was so tiny anyway you could hardly fit a bicycle in there. (Actually, that's exactly what he *did* store there.) He had no idea whatsoever how to cook, so I guess it's lucky he had no interest, either. The only alternative was to take us out to eat. Fortunately, I was chosen to be the de facto designated dining consultant. To help me make decisions, he handed me Craig Claiborne's *New York Times* book of restaurant reviews and told me to pick a place to go as long as it wasn't what he called a "clip joint," his parlance for "ripoff."

This was the perfect setup—a new place every night—and New York is not exactly short on great restaurants to choose from. This job introduced me to a whole new world of tastes, some sophisticated, some simple: my first chicken scarpariello at Forlini's, sophisticated Chinese food at Shun Lee Dynasty, and the iconic thin-crust pizzas at the now defunct Rocky Lee's. Psychologists might suggest that food was a way to ameliorate my emotional pain, but I prefer to think of ameliorate as "a meal you rate."

Then I moved on to college in Bethlehem, Pennsylvania, which was a culinary wasteland at that point with one exception—the "*Greekers*," the name for the local hot dogs served with yellow mustard, chopped onions, melted cheese, and some mysterious,

but oddly tasty, brown sauce with unidentifiable lumps. I would always have two, accompanied by a bag of BBQ potato chips, all washed down with cold Yoo-Hoo chocolate drink. It's the kind of meal you can best appreciate after you've spent an evening consuming vast quantities of punch spiked with 190-proof grain alcohol. I can't figure out if I long for those days or if I'd rather never relive a single one.

After college I moved into Manhattan and went into the advertising business, which added immensely to my eating-out experience. Because I worked on big-budget accounts, it was in the interest of media companies, who wanted to sell our clients their TV ad time or space in their publications, to entertain us. So they took us to lunch almost every day, usually at one of New York City's top restaurants. I had steak and lobster at the Palm, pasta primavera at Il Nido, and caviar and blinis at the Russian Tea Room. You name it, I ate it. For a time I was running four to five miles a day just to burn off a few calories. Even so, by the end of that year, I had gained about twenty pounds.

My professional adventure as an international advertising executive had one more advantage: it took me around the world, and I can tell you firsthand that there are fabulous foods to be found everywhere. I amassed about three million frequent flier miles and ate in over three thousand restaurants with friends and business associates, because one of the first things you do in most any new locale is bond over food. In addition, I learned a lot about the differences in cultures and their cuisines from the warm and impressive people I met and the food we shared, which gives me a pretty rich perspective to share.

Among the many highlights I remember from overeating around the globe: just-baked *empanadas* in Buenos Aires, biltong with gin and tonic in the African bush, conch fritters in the Caribbean, roast chicken in Paris that brought tears to my eyes, killer moules frites in Belgium, steaming and succulent porchetta with crackling skin on freshly baked bread in Italy, the joyful revelation of grilled hearts of palm in Brazil, roasted and shredded duck in hot homemade tortillas in Mexico City with tequila and sangrita, reindeer (yes, reindeer) prepared every way imaginable in Sweden, sweet stone crabs in Miami, and breathtaking barbecue oysters in Northern California that make me want to move there.

I had always enjoyed cooking, but I really wanted to excel at it, anticipating that at some point I'd want to go into the food business. By the time I enrolled in a professional cooking program at night, I had already been in the advertising business for about fifteen years. I chose classical French training because of its structure and discipline. The class met three nights a week after work and lasted five to six hours a night. We chopped, sliced, sautéed, braised, and roasted all manner of French food, which we would sit down to enjoy at the end of the session. I loved every second of the learning, the training, and of course, the tasting. I did my required externship at the fledgling Food Network, assisting producers in preparing the cooking segments on the nightly live show hosted by Robin Leach (of *Lifestyles of the Rich and Famous* fame).

But I have to say, that of all my food-related experiences, nothing is greater or more profoundly rewarding than feeding my family and friends. These are my favorite people in the world and I do my best cooking for them. Now my mission is to share the joy of making great tasting meals with you and the people in your life. And to bring the fun to food.

You *Can* Stand the Heat

The Reason More Men Don't Cook

Cooking for my family has turned out to be one of the most rewarding and bonding experiences of fatherhood, so I am surprised at how many men still actively avoid the kitchen. After all, when it comes to outdoor grilling, we men seem to be in our element. I mean, what guy doesn't get a thrill out of throwing down coals, dousing them with lighter fluid, and setting them ablaze? Why is that such a rush? Is the exhilaration of witnessing flames drilled into our DNA? Or is it simply that inhaling the sweet scent of charring meat takes us back to our caveman ancestry?

How is it that while we are masters at the grill, we seem to be intimidated by the stove? In my opinion, these are the reasons men can't stand the heat in the kitchen:

1. Recipes are like driving directions—and we all know how guys respond to those. We need to understand basic concepts first and then work out the rest on our own.

2. Men don't like unfamiliarity. In fact, we cannot tolerate the state of "not knowing." So, unless you were lucky enough to have a mother or father who took you into the kitchen and taught you the way around, these are uncharted waters. It's like being lost in the jungle. (See reason 1 for why we can't get out of the jungle.)

3. Men are terrified of being judged incompetent. Not only about cooking; it applies to pretty much every aspect of life. It's a fate worse than being denied sex (but not as bad as being judged incompetent at sex).

4. Fear of failure. Cooking is a brand-new endeavor for many of us and it's possible that we won't be any good at it. If there's one thing men hate, it's failure. For me, I'd like to be able to do yoga, but I feel like the village idiot in one of those classes when I can't "bow to the sun." While others stand on their heads with grace and ease, I would twist and contort like a Bavarian pretzel in a pool of my own anxious sweat.

5. Bros are often commitment phobic. But cooking doesn't take nearly as much time as foreplay. Believe me, you can whip up an orgasmic omelet in the same time it takes to toast a frozen waffle.

6. And ultimately, there's the anxiety that dares not speak its name: fear of the feminine. Though a majority of the world's top chefs are still men, somehow, dudes still associate oven mitts with elbow-length gloves. Frankly, it seems far more acceptable for women to assume masculine roles than it is for men to assume the feminine. If cooking appeals to you, you need to get over the association that it's women's work. It's Mario Batali, Gordon Ramsey, and Jamie Oliver's work too, and they are definitely not women.

The Many Benefits of Cooking

Cooking is creative.

There are two distinct parts to the food experience. One is the eating; the other is cooking. On the eating side, which is generally passive, we often tend to grab what's easily available, whether it's from the can, out of the box, or on a menu. But on the cooking side, which is active, we have the opportunity to deviate, elevate, and add excitement to our eating experience. And it doesn't take a lot to do—just a little know-how and some basic principles, which I'll teach you in this book.

Generally, guys open a cookbook and what they see is a recipe with a list of ingredients; of course, this looks complicated right away. But it doesn't have to be that way. Ingredients can be your friends—if you know how to work with them. Whether it's Indian or Italian, savory or sweet, using veggies or meat, the kitchen is a studio and food is the palette.

You can take simple, raw ingredients, and by mixing them together in a certain fashion and proportion, and then generally applying fire to them—voilà, you transform them into a work of art. You are limited only by your imagination and your own willingness to experiment and play. Everything you eat that is by now totally familiar didn't exist at one point. Someone, somewhere had to be the first to ground up steak to make hamburgers, slice potatoes and fry them in oil to make French fries, scramble eggs to make an omelet, bake cookies with chocolate chips in them, put tomato sauce and cheese on top of bread and call it pizza. These were all acts of creation. Unless you're into the raw food movement—people buy sprouted brown gaba rice and eat it as is—then almost every single thing you put in your mouth was at some time "created." Why can't you be a creator, too? Once you learn the basics of cooking, you can envision greatness everywhere you look. Even Elvis Presley, famous for his music, was inventive enough in the kitchen to come up with fried peanut-butter-and-banana sandwiches. Perhaps not to everybody's taste, but they say his friends all loved it.

There are two different kinds of cooks: Those who work from a cookbook and those who fly by the seat of their pants. Many people wouldn't even think of whipping up dinner without a cookbook. Personally, that's not who I am. I might start with a recipe and read it for inspiration, ideas, or general concepts, but then I close the book, put it away, and go to work. However, even if you are more comfortable cooking from a recipe, you can still improvise and adjust the dish. But to do that, you have to become familiar with certain concepts and techniques. If you cook intuitively, as I do, the whole experience allows you to choose from a realm of foods and to combine then in any way you want; in other words, to invent. Isn't that the essence of creativity?

Nobody is going to take you out back and shoot you if you don't stick to a recipe strictly; what you do with one is up to you. As I said, though, you need to understand some basics first before you can be creative and still come up with a meal that tastes good. There is such a thing as overdoing it. For instance, you really wouldn't add mayonnaise to beef stew. Ultimately, the flavors have to work together. But that's learnable. My advice: start small, play around, and feel free to make mistakes. Who knows? You might be the guy who invents the next Buffalo chicken wings, fettuccine Alfredo, or Caesar salad. But to create, you gotta get into the kitchen and learn your way around.

Cooking is rewarding.

Sure, there is a great sense of accomplishment in making something out of nothing, like turning even the simplest eggs into a masterwork of scrambled goodness. But aside from the accolades you'll get for your brilliant new sandwich concoction, it's the pure pleasure of working with ingredients that can be exciting. Just handling them is delicious. Think about how beautiful vibrant yellow and fire-engine red peppers are, or violet-colored Japanese eggplant, or the vivid green of fresh spring peas. When you were a child, remember the feeling of wet sand as you built a sand castle—how good it felt? It's the same with mixing up a mound of meat with your hands to make meat loaf. How about the smell of food: fresh bread right out of the oven, onions caramelizing slowly in melted butter, an apple pie with cinnamon being baked? Just close your eyes and imagine eating your favorite food in the world. Food is pretty to look at, sensual to touch, intoxicating to smell, and naturally, a joy to eat. You'll find that making it isn't work at all; it's kind of sexy.

Food is fun.

Most guys like to work with their hands. Some guys tune cars, and some love to work with wood, whereas others like to grow plants out of the soil. I enjoy cutting, chopping, and slicing vegetables and meat. Some guys like to paint walls, pitch tents, or play guitar; I like to paint sauce on ribs, smear roasted garlic on a just-grilled baguette, rub savory spices into supple meat, sprinkle seasoning on crispy, hot potatoes, and blend the perfect margarita. Some men are excited about tools, whether it's a new buzz saw, pitching wedge, or fishing tackle; I exult in the latest nonstick pan or citrus juicer. Some like the crisp crack of a baseball off a bat; I get a thrill from the sound of the sizzle as meat hits hot oil. Some seek the scent of the surf; I savor the smell of onions slowly sautéing in butter. Some like to shop at Home Depot; I'm a kid in a candy shop at a restaurant supply store. The whole experience of cooking is exhilarating. Yes, I think you should "play with your food."

Clearly, food is more to me than just a basic necessity of life. As I said, I believe in a simple philosophy: Never waste a meal™. Whether it's finding a slice of heaven in a slice of pizza or experiencing sexual satisfaction from a slab of steak or even savoring the simple pleasure of a peach or sensing bliss from the burnt bits of barbecued brisket, "never waste a meal" means that three times a day, every day, you should revel in the food you eat.

Cooking is a bonding experience.

Cooking for others is a gift, but it's especially gratifying when it's for the people you care most about. Dads would do anything for their kids. Like most fathers, I would do anything for mine . . . except make one more trip to Disney World. One of the things I do for them every day is prepare their meals. That's why they're the ones who named me "Short Order Dad." And when they enthusiastically polish off a plate of something I've made and tell me how much they enjoyed it, I am as triumphant as if I just won the lottery. Lamentably, just not as rich. There is no pleasure greater than bringing pleasure to those you love. I do my best cooking for them and it comes effortlessly. And that's because it's not work—it's love.

Cooking is good for your sex life.

Food is not just the way to a man's heart, for it works even better on a woman's. Developing some cooking chops can make your girlfriend, partner, or wife very, very happy. She is far more likely to appreciate even a periodic attempt at preparing her a meal than she would your taking another trip for fast food or nuking up a container of frozen beef Stroganoff. It is attractive to mothers, especially, when you show that you care. They find it sexy when you cook for your kids too. And you know where that leads.

Cooking is healthy.

It lets you manage what goes into your body and your kids'. How important is it to you what your kids eat? You don't need extensive research to tell you that most parents want their little ones to eat better, healthier foods. "Eat your vegetables" has been a popular refrain since Adam and Eve. But serving vegetables to kids

today is more complicated for a couple of reasons. One is that kids seem to have an innate aversion to vegetables and other healthy foods. They're just born into despising broccoli. (That can change: see page 173.) Secondly, we live in a fast-food culture driven by the cheap and the convenient, rather than the wholesome and the nutritious. So no one should be surprised that childhood obesity is an issue. There is, however, one solution to both of these problems: prepare their meals yourself. It's amazing what you can do to cauliflower, for example, to render it great tasting. Plus, you get the extra advantage of sitting down together with your family for the meal. That's more than just a luxury these days; it's incredibly important to their well-being. Research shows that kids eat healthier when they're with their family. When they're out with their friends, they overeat and they consume more crap, which only contributes to the wave of obesity.

Making the Kitchen a Playroom

I'm a pretty typical guy. I like women. I enjoy sports. And I'm good at having mindless fun. But the difference is I know food. Although the number of women working and the number of men cooking is at a historic high, too many still don't get into the game at all, while others are only attempting the most basic and low-level tasks, like boiling something in a plastic bag that looks like wet garbage or microwaving a TV dinner. That's where this book comes in. You don't have to become a great chef (although you probably could). And you certainly don't have to be perfect; that's Martha Stewart's job. My hope is to provide you with a level of competence to create your own culinary successes so that you're able to experience firsthand the satisfaction of serving good eats to the people you love.

I'll offer basic instructions and simple recipes. *I'll show you how to get the most flavor with the least effort and the fewest ingredients.* That's especially important to us guys because we don't like things fussy or froufrou. (Frankly, I don't even know what *froufrou* means, or if I've even spelled it correctly. It just sounds girly.) The point is that my approach is to keep things basic and simple, yet still make it good.

My job is to offer encouragement, particularly to those who don't know what they're missing by not preparing the occasional meal. (At the very least, when you cook, you earn the right to have someone else clean up your mess.) I believe the kitchen is your playroom and you have complete permission to play in it. Sometimes you'll screw up, like we all do. In fact, you need to. First of all, you can't really learn if you don't make mistakes.

Second, that's where half of the fun comes in. Even if you can't recover when it seems like all is lost, it's okay to give up on this round and order pizza. Your effort will still be appreciated. And there's no such thing as bad pizza.

Unless you're being paid to cook, don't be afraid to make mistakes.

I'll also show you the tools of trade. Guys love tools, whether they're from the hardware store or the sports store. (Chances are that whenever you see someone wearing a tool belt, nine times out of ten, it's a guy. Women generally wear much better looking belts.) Some guys are handy with the tools of plumbing, gardening, and painting. Others can tune their own car or piano. But for some reason, men see the tools of the

Never Waste a Meal™

11

kitchen as a completely different animal, not really masculine. But why should that be? A tool is a tool. Think of it this way: you're already using some of the fundamental tools of the sport (and some techniques too) for the barbecue grill as you will indoors. So it's not that much of a stretch to bring your game inside and familiarize yourself with the tools of the kitchen.

And while you're at it, if you're going to make the kitchen a playroom, bring the tunes. Whether Beethoven or Beastie Boys, the "Boss" or the Beatles, Ed Sheeran or EDM is your thing, get a sound track going while you cook. Make music a part of making dinner . . . and chop to the beat.

"Food is music to the body, music is food to the heart."
—Gregory David Roberts

CHAPTER TWO

HOW TO BUILD A PANTRY

You don't literally have to build a pantry. This is a cooking book, not a primer on carpentry. And doesn't *pantry* seem like such a wussy word anyway? How about *cabinet* or *cupboard*, or even *a closet for foodstuff*. The idea, in any case, is that there are certain items you should keep on hand so you can always throw something together that's appetizing to eat.

You're going to want to have foods that are packaged in cans, boxes, and containers for a long shelf life. The ideal list should be composed of ingredients that immediately add flavor impact to anything else you might have lying around, so that's where various condiments and sauces come in handy. You'll also want to include foods that can be transformed directly into a meal, like pasta, even when nothing else is available in your home. And although it's not technically your pantry, there are a number of suggestions here for what to keep in the refrigerator as well.

- **Condiments:** soy sauce, hot sauce (try sriracha, and Korean chile paste *gochujang* is cool too), mustard (Dijon would be good), ketchup, Worcestershire sauce
- **Oils:** good olive is indispensable for dressing and drizzling, peanut is good for cooking, as are "neutral" oils (like canola, grapeseed, or safflower), whose absence of flavor and higher "smoke point" is their advantage (i.e., they perform well over higher heat)
- **Sweet and sour:** vinegar, honey, maple syrup, jam, or jelly. Nutella, because Nutella. Chocolate chips (not necessarily to cook with, but to pop into your mouth occasionally)
- **Cans:** tomatoes (whole, peeled, or chopped; Italian San Marzanos are lovely, if available), beans, tuna fish, tomato paste
- **Boxes:** Pasta, rice, stock (chicken, vegetable, and/or beef), kosher and/or high-quality (Maldon) sea salt!
- **Other:** olives, capers, nuts, peanut butter, raisins, bread crumbs, aromatics (such as onions, garlic, and carrots, which last pretty long), and potatoes are always good to have around
- **Refrigerator:** eggs, cheese (such as Parmesan and cheddar), bacon, butter, tortillas, and lemons!!!
- **Freezer:** peas, spinach, breads, bagged fruits (for smoothies), pizza (for when you mess up)
- **Dried herbs:** such as oregano, thyme, rosemary, tarragon
- **Dried spices:** such as cinnamon, nutmeg, cumin, paprika, chili powder, curry powder, cayenne, peppercorns, red pepper flakes

When Picky is Good: Ingredient Shopping

Here's the thing: you don't go into any new endeavor without first having to learn some of the basics. I don't know much of anything about hang gliding, but you can bet I wouldn't be giving it a whirl unless I first had some idea of what I was doing and how to do it. Exhilaration aside, I have very little interest in free-falling through midair before smashing face-first into a mountainside. It's somewhat the same when it comes to cooking, albeit much less dangerous. The point is that there are a few simple ideas you want to understand before you proceed.

Before we dive into the essential techniques, there's one fundamental rule that I strongly believe and follow. In fact, if I have a mantra in cooking, it's this: *get the best ingredients you can. And don't screw 'em up too much.* Nothing has more impact of the taste on your food than the quality of the ingredients you put into it. And, the better the ingredients you start with, the less you need and want to do with them. For example, there are many ways I will show you to prepare delicious meat and fish, but it's true that an outstanding piece of steak requires nothing more than fire and a little salt to be mouthwatering, and a piece of raw tuna, snapper, or yellowtail with a dip into soy sauce alone can be ethereal.

> "Get the best ingredients you can. And don't screw 'em up too much."

In almost everything we eat—indeed, in every aspect of life—there is a range that runs from poor to extraordinary. Just as there is standout steak and sushi, so too are there disappointments. And what makes one relatively simple dish vastly superior to another is what was used to make it and how it was made. We can practice the making part, and even get really good at it. But as far as the ingredient part—get the best you can. Sometimes best might mean the freshest; other times it might be the more expensive. Most of the time, though, it simply means knowing what to look for when you go shopping.

Choosing Ingredients

There are some cases where particular ingredients will make little difference to the final product. For example, there are numerous brands of expensive butters now available on the market. Some are imported. Some have a higher percentage of fat, which is purported to make a higher quality butter. Feel free to sample fancy butters and see if you discover a discernible difference yourself. However, in general, your cooking is going to be perfectly fine with normal, everyday butter. (Land O'Lakes Unsalted Sweet Butter is considered the standard among most cooks.) The only advice I'd give here is to buy the unsalted variety because salt is an extremely important taste component, so it is essential that *you* control the amount of it in your cooking.

Olive oils, on the other hand, can make a significant difference to the end product. Extra-virgin olive oils do cost more than regular olive oil, but they are worth it because they taste better. And when you are making a dish with few ingredients, each ingredient stands out more, so you're going to want to work with the good stuff. Fresh tomatoes and mozzarella that are topped with nothing more than salt and olive oil call for the best tasting olive you can afford. It can either elevate the dish, or render it dreary. There is no one "best," so the only way to determine quality levels is to taste and compare. Most grocery stores now stock a pretty good variety,

and often specialty food stores provide a little sampling station for tasting. There are terrific olive oils available here from all over the world, especially from the Mediterranean, Italy, Spain, and France. From the supermarket, I like the Monini and Columela brands.

What's an Extra Virgin? The difference between extra-virgin olive oil and regular old olive oil is that extra-virgin is obtained from the first pressing of the olives. (You'll often see the words *First Cold Pressed* on the bottle label.) As a result, it has a more pronounced, pungent flavor than ordinary olive oil does. Does that make a difference? And is it worth the price premium? The short answer is yes. And when the olive oil is a central component of a dish or a sauce, you should use the best you can. When you're making spaghetti with nothing more than oil and garlic, for example. Same thing when you're dipping a crusty piece of baguette into a little bowl of it.

Vinegars: The chances are that you're using the same vinegar over and over. I know people who pour balsamic vinegar on

top everything they eat. You need to know that there is a mesmerizing variety of vinegars out there. For example, there's the nutty-tasting sherry wine vinegar, champagne wine vinegar, apple cider vinegar, rice wine vinegar, and vinegars flavored with herbs. In the category of "you get what you pay for," there is aged balsamic vinegar, which can run you upward of a hundred bucks a bottle, but whose sweetness and syrupy texture is incomparable on top of freshly sliced strawberries or a chunk of Parmigiano-Reggiano cheese, for example. The point is, go explore and taste different vinegars if you can, because each has its own characteristics that can have a profound impact on the dish you're making.

Fruits and vegetables are almost always preferable to purchase fresh rather than the canned and frozen products. They taste better. Their texture is better. And they haven't been altered in any way—as they might when canned or frozen—which makes them more nutritious, too. Peaches in a can are mighty tasty (generally because they're stored in sweet syrup), but if you've ever had a peach at its peak of ripeness in midsummer, its heavenly juice dripping from your chin, you know what I'm talking about here. Go fresh whenever you can; it will make your meals better.

Of course there are some exceptions, too: frozen peas are terrific, frozen fruit is ideal for kids' smoothies and dads' daiquiris, and I use canned beans often in my kitchen. And most chefs agree that canned tomatoes, especially from the San Marzano region of Italy, make a sauce as good, or sometimes better, than fresh ones. But whenever you can, get your fruit and veggies fresh, in their natural state, and as close to the source as you can. Fresh produce, in season, continues to be a revelation. Just-picked corn on the cob is so sweet you can enjoy it raw. As are fresh berries, pineapple, asparagus, cherries, greens, basil, and so many others.

Potatoes: There are many types of potatoes, but for cooking purposes, all you generally need to know is that they fall into two categories—starchy and waxy—and that some varieties work better for certain dishes

than others. The starchy ones (like Idaho/Russet) are ideal for baking because they get light and kind of fluffy when cooked. They also make good fries. The thinner, smoother-skinned "waxy" kind of potato, often red, yellow, and round, are good for boiling and steaming and ideal for soups and dishes like potato salad because they hold their shape well. For mashed potatoes, I like Yukon Gold for their creamy taste and texture. To bake, I'll take Idaho. I like the way they can be simultaneously soft on the inside, yet crisp on the outside. Fingerling potatoes are kind of smallish, which means they don't take as long to cook, so they come out very well in a sauté or roasted with olive oil. Potatoes also come in a rainbow of colors, like purple, which makes for some very pretty food.

Beef: The US Government grades steak, so clearly there are varying levels of quality that are determined by flavor and texture. USDA Prime is the best (only about 2–3 percent of all beef achieves this superior rating); USDA Choice comes next (most of the higher quality grocery stores carry this); and then comes

USDA Select (which is generally found everywhere else). Some steaks are aged for many days to improve their tenderness and intensify their flavor. The good news is that steak does not have to be prohibitively expensive to taste wonderful. In fact, some of the most flavorful cuts can also be the least expensive, like a skirt steak or short ribs. But you need to know how to best prepare those to coax out the most flavor possible, which we will cover in the chapter on techniques.

Poultry: I'm no fan of the popular supermarket brands of chicken. I find them bland and rubbery. And if you've seen the alarming documentary *Food, Inc.,* you might not want to eat mass-produced chicken ever again. However, if you can get your hands on a kosher, organic, or free-range bird, they're generally better. You can instantly taste the difference.

As for turkey, I've had perfectly fine results with the good old frozen kind. Kosher turkeys have already been brined (which means soaked in a saltwater solution), so they come with built-in flavor. I think duck is totally underappreciated and underused by the home cook, but I am a great fan of it, particularly cooking the breast. Most duck breasts are sold frozen, and if you buy them that way, make sure what you're buying is boneless with skin, and raw, not smoked or precooked. Again, I prefer fresh, in which case you'll be looking for a Pekin, Moulard, or Muscovy duck breast.

Fish and seafood: Fresh. Fresh. Fresh. Few things are as unappealing, even disgusting, to eat when they aren't fresh. The best idea is to get it from a fishmonger in a fish or seafood store, or to buy it from a market with very high turnover that receives their deliveries daily. In fact, don't be afraid to ask someone in charge when the fish you're planning to buy was delivered. One of the best ways to tell if fish is fresh is—are you ready for this?—when it doesn't smell like fish. That's right. Fresh fish should be free of smell, or perhaps have a mild ocean-like odor. Use your nose. If it doesn't smell good, it won't improve with cooking and it won't taste good.

Although the advantage to buying fish whole is getting freshness and taste at the best price, it is much easier to cook boneless fillets or whole pieces of fish called "steaks." If you do buy whole fish, look for bright, clear eyes—neither dull or hazy—and skin that's moist and shiny, with firm flesh. When purchasing fillets and steaks, look for moist flesh and skin that is shiny and resilient. If the color is dull or browning, don't buy it.

Cheese: One could write an entire book on cheese, but that won't be me. It is far too large a category to comment on in detail, yet there are some basic principles to know. There are hundreds of types of cheeses, which are generally categorized as follows:

- **Fresh:** Smooth, creamy, and mild tasting, like ricotta, feta, mozzarella, cottage, and cream cheese.
- **Soft:** Camembert, Brie, goat cheese.
- **Semisoft:** These have a rind and range in taste from sweet and buttery (Edam, Pont l'Évêque) to more aromatic (Epoisses).
- **Semi-hard:** Provolone, Gouda, and Jarlsberg are examples.
- **Hard:** Cheddar, Parmigiano-Reggiano, Gruyère, and Manchego are some of the best known.
- **Blue:** These cheeses (Stilton, Roquefort, Gorgonzola, and Maytag Blue) have blue "veins" running through them, which gives them a sharp, salty (and acquired) taste.

The more that the cheese is the star of a dish, as opposed to a supporting player, the more you'll probably want to invest in the best version of that cheese you can. For example, pizza with basic grocery store mozzarella is fine, but is improved by freshly made mozzarella. Grilled cheese sandwiches with slices of American will do, but can be upgraded significantly by choosing a cheese with character.

Unless you're feeling lazy and cash-rich, grate your own. The grated Parmesan that comes in a cardboard container will never match the flavor you get from freshly grated Parmigiano-Reggiano. Although Parmigiano-Reggiano is a more expensive investment, you don't have to use as much of it because it has a rich full, flavor. Other than for pure convenience, it doesn't make sense to buy already grated cheese for which you pay a premium when it is quite easy to grate yourself, and it will be fresher, too.

Different cheeses, naturally, serve different purposes. Cheddar, Swiss, Muenster, provolone, jack, and mozzarella are all good choices when you need cheese that melts well. As is good old processed American. For grating, hard cheeses like Parmesan, Pecorino, and Grana are ideal. For straight up enjoying with a glass of wine, I'm always happy with a chunk of Gruyère or Parmigiano-Reggiano, known as the "King of Cheeses."

Wine for cooking: Here's the rule: don't cook with any wine you wouldn't drink. That means never buy "cooking wine" in the supermarket. Wine adds flavor and depth to many a dish. Most of the alcohol itself evaporates and what's left behind is the concentrated character of the grape. That could be sweetness, richness, tartness, earthiness, or fruitiness, depending on the wine, the rest of the ingredients, and when in the cooking process

it is added. When you're using it as the cooking medium or vessel, like pears poached in red wine or mussels steamed in white wine, wine goes in at the beginning. When it's being used to "deglaze" or make a sauce, wine goes in at the end. But whether it's a traditional *boeuf Bourguignon* (beef braised in red wine), classic coq au vin (chicken cooked in wine), or just a splash of vino in your tomato sauce, wine adds a dimension of flavor and sophistication like nothing else.

Although I wouldn't go so far as to suggest you buy an expensive bottle of wine to cook with, do purchase a wine that you would gladly serve with the meal. In fact, it is not unusual to use the same wine in cooking that you will be drinking. For example, I steam clams in Pinot Gris while my guest and I are enjoying a glass of the same.

Pasta: Nowhere in this book will I instruct you in how to make your own fresh pasta. (Perhaps I will show you in the next book, when you'll be ready.) That's because of what I call the *effort to enjoyment ratio*. Specifically, that refers to the relationship between

the amount of time and effort it takes to make something and the pleasure it yields. So in the case of making your own fresh pasta noodles, the degree of effort and time necessary to get it done well (coupled with your investment in a pasta making machine that you're not likely to use all that often) will not deliver sufficiently more value than buying a box of pasta from the supermarket shelf. To be clear, fresh pasta is fantastic to eat due to its silky, supple, and luxurious mouthfeel. But you can order it in a restaurant or purchase some directly from a store that makes it fresh rather than attempt to make your own. For the most part, you'll do very well with standard boxed pasta, particularly if all you plan to do is dump a bottle of premade marinara over your noodles. (But don't do that; I'll show you how to make your own on page 149.) As for the stuff that comes in the box, as far as I can tell, it's all pretty much the same. Barilla, Ronzoni, and DeCecco all make good products.

Be aware that different shapes of pasta—long, short, thick, thin, ridged, smooth, curved, and with crevices—should be matched with certain sauces to obtain maximum results. There is a reason you always see linguini with clam sauce on a menu. It's that the right shape blends harmoniously with its sauce, the wrong one leaves something to be desired. The more delicate fresh pasta goes best with more subtle sauces, whether they're made with vegetables, seafood, or meat, which are often butter-based and enriched with cream. Dry, boxed pasta is more hearty and substantial, so it can better handle the bolder, thicker, and chunkier sauces. For example, penne works well for a simple tomato sauce, and rigatoni would be ideal with meat sauce. The long, thin pasta, such as spaghetti or capellini, pairs well with olive oil based sauces. The thicker fettuccine and tagliatelle stand up nicely to cream sauces, as does the corkscrew shaped fusilli. Just remember that there should be harmony between your pasta and your sauce. In the recipe section, I'll help do the matching for you.

Speaking of pasta, let's head back to the principle with which we started the chapter: "get the best ingredients you can. And don't screw 'em up too much." Italian cuisine, in general, provides many good examples of how one can make a seriously delicious dish with a few simple, quality components that require minimal cooking and handling. Take *spaghetti aglio e olio*, for example. It's a classic pasta dish made with three primary ingredients: spaghetti, olive oil, and garlic (to which you will eventually add salt, pepper, and grated cheese). When it's made properly, with very good olive oil, these three simple ingredients combine together to become, as they say, greater than the sum of their parts. However, making it well takes a little understanding and practice. One

has to know how to ensure that the pasta is "al dente," meaning cooked to the proper texture so that it has a little chew to it. (Guys especially can appreciate that "soft" or "limp" are not favorable attributes; you must think of your pasta the same way.) And the garlic needs to be lightly and perfectly browned so as to release its full flavor without exposing its bitterness. Also, perhaps, how much of the pasta cooking water itself might be necessary to add back to the garlic oil "sauce," so that it binds properly to the noodles and yields even distribution of sauce per noodle. No one wants some noodles naked while others are drenched in sauce. This is all relatively easy to do, but very important to the outcome of the dish. That's where understanding technique comes into play, as well as knowing what not to do.

CHAPTER THREE

RECIPES FOR DISASTER* (OR WHAT NOT TO DO)

Now that you have your best ingredients on hand, here comes the other part of the equation: DON'T MESS THEM UP TOO MUCH. It's obvious that you can screw up perfectly good ingredients if you don't know what to do with them. However, whereas a lot of books will tell you what to do, I believe it is just as important to understand what not to do. My advice is clear: don't try to do too much. In fact, generally speaking, the less you do with them, the better. What I have often found in my experience is that most of the mistakes that people make—and this goes for amateur chefs as well as professionals—come from the tendency to try to do too much. That goes for overcooking, over-seasoning, over-saucing, too many ingredients, and too much handling. The DON'Ts are just as important as the DO's.

Life is complicated enough. Your meals shouldn't have to be.

* There's really no disaster in cooking. But you will surely minimize the chance for culinary catastrophe—particularly when cooking for an eager crowd—if you keep some of these thoughts in mind.

DON'T OVERCOOK: This is probably the most common mistake there is. Obviously we need enough heat and fire to make food taste good and to eliminate any potential concerns about bacteria that could arise from undercooked food. HOWEVER, overcooking food often ruins it. Overcooked vegetables become soggy and take on an unappetizing baby food texture. Moreover, it also leaches the vegetables of their nutritional value. Overcooked

proteins—meat, poultry, seafood, and fish—get dried out, plain and simple. They get tough and lose their natural juice, which provides so much of the flavor. There comes a certain point in cooking beyond which you will have sucked out the entire flavor by overcooking. We've probably all had some experience eating food that was dried out by overcooking. For example, I would venture to say that three out of every four Thanksgiving turkeys served in this country are left in the oven for too long.

But it's not just turkey. Overcooked shrimp gets rubbery. Overcooked fish is dry. Pasta becomes mushy. Casseroles lose liquid and turn dense when they dry out. Even desserts fail—for example, soufflés fall—when overdone. And scrambled eggs, too, lose their fluffiness when they're cooked too long. I firmly believe that more people would be eating liver, as polarizing as it is (people just seem to loathe liver), if it was served a little bit pink inside instead of being overcooked to the point where it tastes like, well . . . liver. Overcooked liver tastes metallic and *minerally* and its texture becomes hard and rubbery.

Listen, I understand that people might be concerned about possible illness from undercooking CERTAIN foods, but that doesn't mean everything needs to be cooked to death. I also understand that some people prefer their meat very well done (although I don't understand why). Remember this: if food is too rare you can always return it to the fire. But once you overcook it, you can't go back and recapture the taste, texture, and vitality that you've lost.

DON'T OVERSAUCE: Very simply, this is the act of drowning food in sauce. I imagine people do this because they think the sauce is the star. *Au contraire, mon frère.* It's just the opposite. Other than with certain pasta dishes, your main ingredient is the star and the sauce should be the supporting player.

Sauce and gravy are meant to embellish our food, to enhance a dish's flavor, to highlight your ingredients, not hide them. This applies to salad dressing, pasta sauce, gravy, au jus, or mayonnaise. Look, I like a good gravy as much as the next guy, but if I want soup, I'll order soup. Too much sauce obscures the main ingredient and changes the flavor and character of a dish. It makes food heavy and soggy. A cream sauce or cheese sauce can deaden and overwhelm what's underneath them. Ever have so much mayonnaise in a chicken salad sandwich that you can't taste the chicken? The same rule holds with salad dressing, which is similar to a sauce because it ties all the salad ingredients together. In cooking school, it was a huge no-no to overdress a salad, and yet it's done all the time in restaurants. Not only does it make the ingredients soggy, it covers their true taste.

Another example occurs in eating sushi. Some people insist on dousing the fish with soy sauce, which is naturally very salty. But when you're paying that much for raw fish that's not a flavor you want to mask. If you

like soy sauce so much, you'd be better of dumping it on a bowl of plain rice than overwhelming your sushi with it. (By the way, you should not be dipping your sushi rice in the soy sauce, only the fish part.)

DON'T OVER-SEASON: Salt is more than good. It has been called the world's most essential mineral. In fact, no ingredient is more important to bringing out the flavor of food than salt.

The human tongue is constructed to respond to four tastes: they are sweet (sugar), sour (lemon), bitter (think coffee, beer, dark chocolate), and salt. These are the sensations that excite the tongue, salt being the most common. In recipes, when you read the words "season," as in "season to taste," it generally refers to salt and pepper.

I happen to be a proponent of what is termed "to season aggressively." That is, I use salt and pepper pretty liberally, and will actually "season" with them throughout the making of a recipe, not just when it's complete. So if I'm sautéing some carrots, celery, and onion in preparation for a dish, I will "season" those, and then also sprinkle salt and pepper on whatever other components are added along the way. However, too much of a good thing is still too much, and too much salt can render a dish inedible. Note that salt levels are intensified as liquids reduce, so be conscious of that when adding salt to any reduction.

DON'T USE TOO MANY INGREDIENTS: This is a common problem in home cooking and at restaurants too: there is simply too much going into a dish and too much going onto the plate.

> "Good food is simple food."
> —Jean Anthelme Brillat-Savarin

One of the greatest food writers of all time, Jean Anthelme Brillat-Savarin, put it best when he said, "Good food is simple food." When you think about your favorite foods, I bet most of them are pretty simple.

Too many ingredients in a dish often detract from the main ingredient, taking focus away from the food you want to concentrate on. They can distract the palate, masking the clarity of a flavor rather than enhancing it. A raw oyster, for example, is a thing of beauty

SALT

Taste is entirely subjective. But what's certain is that nothing is more effective at bringing out the taste in food than salt. There are four common varieties: iodized table salt, kosher salt, sea salt, and *fleur de sel* (a type of sea salt). They're all basically sodium chloride, so chemically, there is little difference between them. In fact, chemists think that anyone who would spend big bucks on all the fancy salts available these days are nuts. (But how often do you share nuts with a chemist?) However, there are significant differences in terms of where they come from and how they're processed that not only affects their texture and shape, but importantly, how each interacts with food.

Many recipes that call for salt are referring to table salt. However, most cooks prefer to cook with kosher salt because its coarser grains make it easier to use and disperse, particularly when adding salt to foods with your fingers. And its "flaky" texture makes a better "crust" on meats or fish. It also tends to taste less salty because the fine grain a single teaspoon of table salt contains more salt than a tablespoon of kosher or sea salt. Sea salt comes from evaporating seawater.

Fleur de sel is a type of sea salt that is harvested by hand; its high mineral content often makes it smell of the sea. Sea salts are best used to sprinkle on food at the last minute for a salty crunch.

FYI: If you oversalt a soup, drop a cut up raw potato into it to absorb the salt. Cream will whip better if you add a pinch of salt. And egg whites will beat faster and higher if you add a pinch of salt.

whose essence-of-the-sea taste could easily be enjoyed alone. It might be highlighted with a splash of lemon, perhaps a dash of hot sauce or a vinegar-based mignonette sauce, but it doesn't need more to reveal its flavor. Furthermore, too many ingredients give you a greater chance of messing things up. Of course there are many exceptions to this rule. You can't make a decent paella or jambalaya, for example, without a whole load of ingredients. But this book is for people who don't regularly make their own paella. Remember, we're here to get the most flavor with the *fewest ingredients and the least effort* ™.

> "The ambition of every good cook must be to make something very good with the fewest possible ingredients."
> —Urbain Dubois

To be clear, I'm not suggesting that you can't make extraordinary food with a ton of ingredients. I am saying that you don't need a ton of ingredients to make extraordinary food. The point is that there are

too many dishes made with too many ingredients that often don't improve it, but complicate it unnecessarily. This "everything but the kitchen sink" approach to cooking more times than not diffuses the attention of your taste buds to the point where it's hard to discern what you're eating.

My experience is that a successful dish should focus on a main component and use the other ingredients to enhance its flavor. Think of it as a football team; there is only one quarterback who leads the team. Let's use shrimp as the example. The shrimp is the quarterback, and we need the rest of the squad to help carry us into the end zone of shrimp scampi. The offensive line is the butter, the fullback handles the garlic, the receivers will bring the white wine and lemon juice, while the halfback completes the play with his parsley, salt, and pepper moves. The quarterback calls the play and the whole team works together to score a touchdown!

Most taste. Fewest ingredients. Least effort™.

Just as importantly, who wants to cook with so many ingredients anyway? A lot of ingredients generally means a lot more steps in the cooking process, which can be more complicated to manage. It means a lot of measuring and a lot of pans, too. When I see recipes that require too many more than seven or eight key ingredients, I either skip them or try to find ways to re-create them with fewer. Ideally, the fewer ingredients I have to work with, the better. Sure, more can be better. And while you should definitely enjoy the occasional beef Wellington and other complex fare that takes fifteen to twenty ingredients to make, leave that work to the professionals for now. I bet that when you think about your favorite foods, most of the time they're pretty simple.

DON'T OVERHANDLE: The closer you get to food in its natural state, the better. The more it's handled, the more you alter the food's natural goodness. Think about freshly picked strawberries. They're delicate little creatures. You can slice them and you can cook them, but you're not going to meaningfully improve upon them from when they're at their peak of natural flavor.

Guys like to play, and although I encourage playing with your food, you must avoid the temptation to do more than needs to be done, particularly if you are relatively new to cooking. Few foods are improved by more handling. You'll notice this often when it comes to cooking over fire. People feel the need to turn food over constantly and move it around incessantly. Not only is that unnecessary, it's actually detrimental, because it doesn't allow the food to develop properly and often causes precious moisture to escape. As a general rule, you should let one side cook all the way, and then flip it over only one time. And, as any baker will tell you, overworking a dough can make baked goods too dense and chewy.

Before we start cooking, let's talk tools.

Tool Talk
(It Helps to Have the Right Gear)

Let's be honest: you're willing to spend a thousand bucks on a set of good golf clubs despite your handicap. You bought that hundred-dollar Nike softball glove for your weekend league. So if you want to be considered a decent cook, you've got to buy some serious gear. And unlike the clubs or the glove, an investment in the kitchen makes you instantly better.

Make the Cut

The place to start is with good knives, beginning with a high-quality chef's knife. Just like that new graphite racket, the most important consideration is how comfortable it feels in your hand. Look for high-carbon, stainless steel, one-piece construction, usually eight to ten inches long. But don't hesitate to buy a six-inch version if it feels better. Remember, it's not the size of your sword, but the manner in which you use it. Wüsthof, Henckels, and Global are well known, but more expensive brand names, whereas Victorinox offers excellent choices for much less.

After the chef's knife, the paring knife is probably the next one to have. It does all of the smaller cutting work that the chef's knife doesn't. That said, I probably use a "utility" knife as much as any knife I have. Running somewhere between four and six inches, a convenient midpoint between a chef and a paring, and can be used for all variety of slicing, dicing and trimming.

Finally, a good serrated knife would be ideal to have if you're going to be slicing a lot of bread. Or cake. Or tomatoes.

Take the Heat

Now, upgrade your cookware. There are two things to know about pots and pans. One is that there is no perfect material. The second is that thickness is the name of the game. Yes, you can scramble an egg on grandma's hand-me-down tin pan, but to boost your game, get some quality pieces blessed with heavy bottoms. Begin with a good-size sauté pan. Cast-iron works well and it's inexpensive. I love the way it holds heat and maximizes crispiness, and that it can be transferred directly from stove top into a waiting hot oven. The thing is it's pretty heavy, which might make it somewhat impractical for everyday cooking. (And make sure you have an oven mitt because that handle gets HOT.) Aluminum is fine if you choose a heavy gauge (try Calphalon). The same holds true for stainless steel, which is best for its longevity. In fact, All-Clad has an excellent portfolio of stainless-steel cookware sets that last longer than most marriages. Great value for the money can be had with the Tramontina 12-inch Tri-Ply Stainless Steel Frying Pan.

Find Utility Players

Stocked with those essentials, it's time to make your cooking experience even easier. Introducing the rest of your team:

- **Tongs**. Grabbing, holding, and pushing are penalties in most sports, but not in the kitchen stadium. Tongs are like handy friends; go for stainless steel with silicone tips.
- **Kitchen scissors (or "shears")**. Underappreciated, but highly useful to cut up chicken, to snip fresh herbs, and also comes in handy to open that corrugated box that FedEx just delivered.
- **Vegetable peeler**. One of those $4.99 numbers. Until you have a sharp one, peeling potatoes will always seem like a prison job.
- **Pepper mill**. If you're still using store-bought pre-ground pepper, it's time to man up

and grind your own. It's a game-changer.

- **Microplane grater.** A versatile, handheld gizmo used to grate fresh cheese, lemon peel, or nutmeg. Best to avoid your fingers, though, as they leave a distinct aftertaste.
- **Whisk**. Stainless steel. Your sauces should be as smooth as you are, lover boy. Now beat it.
- **Instant-read thermometer**. Why worry about undercooked, salmonella chicken or overdone, dried-out roasts? Just stick this little scorekeeper in your beef or bird and you'll know precisely where you stand between well done and rare.
- **Spatula**. Seems obvious, right? Try the offset variety, cantilevered from the handle, making it particularly easy to manipulate inside a curved pan. Or splurge on a flexible one if you plan to cook a lot of fish.
- **Strainer**. Sure, you'll need a colander to drain your pasta, but a small, fine-mesh strainer very often comes in handy for more than just cleaning cannabis. Like lemon juice, for example.
- **Blender**. Some jobs simply call for a power tool. This is

the one you'll want for sauces, soups, dressings, and perhaps most importantly, killer frozen margaritas.

- **Oven mitts**. Good ones that protect your delicate little paws up to 500 degrees or more. Nothing stings quite like scorching skin. (Plus it's much harder to cook with only one good hand.)

Now that you are fully equipped with a deep bench, you are ready to play. You look like a pro, and you're already more confident. Remember, on this field, your sports drink is a big old beer or goblet of wine. Enjoy the game!

It's time to start. Let me tell you about some key principles and basic techniques you'll want to understand so you can get in there and play.

CHAPTER FOUR

LET'S TALK TECHNIQUE: 10 FUNDAMENTALS

You could be a great cook. That starts with understanding some of the basics. These are ten essential techniques you should know about. Even if you don't master all of them, learning any one of these techniques can be the key to turn you on to cooking. You will be able to make dishes and create tastes you were never able to before. And that's with just one technique; imagine what's possible now that I'm going to show you ten of them, which you can learn one at a time, or try several at once. Look, not everybody takes to every kind of cooking method. I discovered from my own cooking school experience that baking didn't really do it for me, but there are plenty of people who are thrilled to be making cupcakes and pastry cream every day. Great. I loved the flames of fire under a pan. The sound of sizzling meats and poultry was music to my ears.

And making sauces for them excited me. So, when a job called for searing, sautéing, or preparing something like a duck breast or a pork loin in a skillet on the stove, that was for me. Start by finding the techniques that are most interesting to you.

There are those who say that the invention of cooking actually drove the evolution of mankind. I don't know about that, but I'm pretty sure that the discovery of fire certainly drove cooking. So, remember that fire is your friend. All due respect to the raw food movement (talk about three words that just should *not* go together—RAW & FOOD & MOVEMENT), there is nothing that transforms food more or better than heat. It changes food's color, texture, form, and flavor. Think about the multiple effects of heat on meat: it shrinks, it gets darker, it softens, and it turns real tasty. Cooking

fruit makes it sweet and soft. With heat, certain other foods will blend together, like fat, flour, and liquid combine to make gravy.

"Cooking is the signature feature of the human diet, and indeed, of human life. It's the development that underpins many other changes that have made humans so distinct from other species."
—Harvard Professor Richard Wrangham

Let's begin with perhaps the most important principle.

1. CARAMELIZATION
In short, it's the browning of food. Scientifically, caramelization is the

process of applying heat to sugar and converting it (by "browning it") into caramel. Now this might come as somewhat of a surprise, but almost all foods—meats, fruits, and vegetables alike—contain some natural sugar. With sufficient heat, starting at about 310°F, sugars break down, resulting in a brown color and a rich flavor. Caramelization, in other words, is the reason why everything from fried onions to grilled steak to *dulce de leche* tastes so damn good.

There may be a whole bunch of fancy words to describe the caramelization process—for example, it's technically called the "Maillard reaction"—but who gives a pork butt? All you need to know is that browning anything from an apple to chicken skin will result in better color and richer, more concentrated flavor. At its very simplest, caramelization is basically what makes food taste good. It's what makes bread look like toast and turns potatoes into golden brown French fries. Of all the benefits that fire brings, this is surely one of the greatest. It is responsible for everything from the taste of perfectly charred steak and crackling chicken skin to caramel itself. And if you've ever held a marshmallow over a campfire, you have already caramelized something and are very familiar with its benefits.

The only utensils you need to caramelize are those that allow foods to come into contact with sufficient heat, but with little moisture: a sauté pan or skillet, a roasting pan for the oven, or a grill. In other words, you won't get the caramelization effect from steaming or boiling.

It is not hard to do, either. If you want to practice caramelizing, simply slice an onion, any way you want. Add enough butter or oil to a frying pan, skillet, or sauté pan to cover the surface of the

Sucs (pronounced suke)

When you brown meat you will undoubtedly notice some brown material accumulating and adhering to the bottom of your pot or pan. These caramelized bits are good. They're called *sucs*. They're loaded with flavor. And that flavor is the basis of many an excellent sauce. Your job, when it comes to *sucs*, is twofold: one is to make sure that you don't burn the stuff. So lower the heat the second you see that your *sucs* might be in danger of burning. Or before that. The other is to deglaze. That is, using liquid to release the *sucs* and form the foundation of a sauce, gravy, or jus.

The best *sucs* are dark-golden brown, and the result of a few key steps. 1) Heat your pan and your lubrication (oil) before adding any ingredients. 2) Do not overcrowd the pan. Overcrowding is a problem in schools; it is also a problem in a pan because it creates steam and liquid rather than *sucs*. 3) Try not to leave too much exposed space between ingredients in the pan because that leaves greater opportunity for burning. Best to make sure you use a pan that is the right size for what you're cooking, or cook in batches. No problem.

pan. (Let's say two tablespoons.) Put on a medium flame, add onions, a pinch of salt, and give an occasional stir. Check back every few minutes to watch how they're changing color. First they'll soften. Then you'll start to notice as they become more translucent. Finally, over time, they'll begin to brown. When they reach the shade of brown you find appealing (browner = better and burnt = bad), congratulate yourself, because you have just successfully caramelized an onion.

Drop it on your burger, mix it into your eggs, or serve it on top of mashed potatoes. In fact, do with it whatever pleases you now that you are officially a caramelizing professional. It is a technique you will use over and over again with fruit, vegetables, and proteins like meat and poultry (not to mention sugar, marshmallows, nuts, fruits, toast, and more). Furthermore, be aware that when you caramelize meats and poultry, the residue that remains in the pan (the *sucs*) is the basis of a truly excellent sauce.

2. DEGLAZING

Deglazing is a fancy term for the technique that takes the browned bits left in the bottom of the pan from caramelizing and dissolves them with liquid. These deposits, called *sucs*, which remain in the pan after proteins like meat or poultry is cooked, are loaded with flavor. (Even the words "browned bits" have me salivating.) The benefit of deglazing is to gather up all that flavor so it can be used to make a great sauce or gravy.

Once the cooked protein and excess fat are removed from the pan, liquid is added—such as water, stock, cream or alcohol—thus allowing you to scrape, dislodge, and dissolve these dark, supercharged pellets of flavor from the bottom of the pan, thereby extracting all the flavor possible. It is common practice to add aromatic vegetables—like onions, shallots, garlic, scallions—to your pan BEFORE YOU ADD THE LIQUID, allowing them to cook briefly, just long enough to release their flavor, which you will happily smell. This adds another dimension to the liquid mixture you're making.

Deglazing the pan is the first step of any one of a number of things you can do with this flavorful liquid, from using it as a sauce itself to making it the base of a more complex sauce. You can season the liquid and serve it just as is, in which case you will have made a quick, flavorful basic sauce known as a jus, as in chicken au jus. You can thicken it by adding some starch (like flour) or smooth out the flavor and texture by whisking in cold butter. You can also thicken it naturally by reducing the liquid over heat, which will create a more intense, concentrated flavor.

It is worth noting that you want to remove excess fat before you start deglazing. Who wants greasy gravy? Too much fat is undesirable because it coats the tongue and obscures flavors. Although much less frequently employed, it is also possible to "deglaze" a pan using vegetables instead of liquid IF they are watery-type vegetables such as onions, celery, or spinach. Their water content will have the same dislodging effect.

For your first attempt, you might try this: remove a beautifully brown chicken from the roasting pan you've cooked it in, strain off the excess fat in the pan, and over heat, stir in a minced clove of garlic and cook until fragrant, about a minute.

Then add a cup of water and stir around vigorously, making sure you scrape up all the brown bits in the bottom until they are dissolved into the liquid. A wooden spoon is best. Keep stirring until the liquid is uniform. It's official: you have just deglazed. Next, taste to see if it needs any salt and pepper. You can pour this flavorful mixture over the chicken as is, and serve chicken au jus, or you can add a variety of other elements to it, from mustard to herbs to butter, and more. You could also keep cooking it until it reaches a thicker consistency. You can strain it before using so it contains no bits of anything floating in it. Ahhh, there you go—not only have you deglazed a pan, you have just completed the first step toward entering the Sauce Making Hall of Fame. You rock star!

3. REDUCTION

Reduction is the process of cooking a liquid mixture to thicken it and intensify its flavor, which is accomplished by the magic of evaporation. The key benefit of reduction is a more concentrated flavor from the liquid you are reducing. Learning how to do this very simple technique will open a whole new world of cooking for you because it allows you to make sauces, gravy, syrup, and more. You will automatically become a better cook because your dishes will have more flavor, better taste, and a more sophisticated flair. Let's face it: many times the sauce makes the dish. Who wants to eat a plain plate of noodles? Some dishes just aren't the same without sauce. That's why this technique expands your cooking prowess immeasurably.

The reduction method is commonly used to make gravies, sauces, and syrups by reducing different liquids— for example, stocks, wine, or milk—depending, of course, on what you're making. Whereas other methods of making sauce might require the addition of thickening agents, such as starches like flour or cornstarch, the thicker consistency you get through reduction is accomplished without any additives. In fact, there are times that liquids are reduced to the thickness of "syrup." The gooey consistency of caramel sauce, for example, is made with sugar and cream that has been reduced down in volume. Any decent wine sauce you've ever had has undoubtedly been achieved through reduction from the time it left the bottle. Reduction produces a richer tasting and smoother product.

As the cook, you control the consistency of the reduction, which can range anywhere from the thinness of apple juice to the thickness of a syrupy glaze like the caramel. That consistency depends on what you're using the liquid for. As in the example I cited before, when roasting a chicken, I will deglaze the roasting pan with a cup of water and reduce that liquid down by about one half to produce a wonderful jus with the natural drippings from the bird. On the other hand, when making Thanksgiving turkey, I want a thicker gravy and a lot more of it, so I will start with about four cups of liquid and reduce it until it yields just one. It is important to remember that the more you reduce a liquid, the more you magnify the flavor(s) of what's in it. So be careful with salt and sugar levels, because what starts out sweet and salty becomes even more so.

There is a direct relationship between the amount of liquid

you begin with and the heat required to reduce it to a desired consistency. A lot of liquid in a pan needs higher heat to reduce it and/or more time. The closer you get to a syrupy glaze, the more you have to moderate and keep your eye on the heat. You can use any stove-top pot to reduce liquids; just make sure that the pot is large enough to hold the amount of liquid you start with.

When deglazing a large roasting pan, like one used for turkey, I begin with the pan over heat on top of the stove and scrape up the brown *sucs*. (It can actually cover two burners simultaneously.) Then, once I have deglazed, I transfer the liquid from this pan to a smaller pot so that I can reduce the liquid over a single flame. Not only does that give me more control, but also allows me to add liquid and any necessary ingredients to build a sauce or gravy. If your only intention is to make a jus, that can be done right in the roasting pan and poured directly over your dish.

If you want to practice, try this: put a half cup of regular, generic balsamic vinegar in a saucepan, add a sprig of thyme, and simmer over medium heat until it gets as thick as maple syrup. There, you've just completed your first reduction. Not only will you see the texture change, but the reduction also accentuates the natural sweetness in balsamic, which creates a good topping to drizzle over vegetables, chicken, or fish. Taste a tiny bit of it on your next piece of plain grilled chicken or asparagus. Or swirl a little bit on the side of a plate as a design. There, now you're a food stylist, too.

A reduction is simply done by cooking down the liquid in a pan until it reaches the volume and consistency you want.

4. BRAISING

Braising is a method of cooking that uses wet heat. You are simmering food in liquid, like water, wine, or stock, over a low heat for a long time, in a tightly covered pot. Braising has also been referred to as pot-roasting and is a similar method to stewing, but in stews the meat is generally cut into even pieces and cooked in enough liquid to cover. Nor is braising the same as poaching, which is a process of gently simmering food in liquid, and is generally used for "gentle" food, hence such dishes as poached eggs and poached salmon. Braising is characterized by long, slow cooking using an amount of liquid that covers about half to two-thirds of the main ingredient. Braising is most often used for tough cuts of meat that need to cook gently until tender. The most common types of foods that are braised are beef, pork, and chicken, as well as vegetables such as leeks, onions, and cabbage.

Even if you've never made it yourself, you've undoubtedly had braised food before in restaurants. You might recognize it from that feeling you get when you're eating something so tender that it "falls right off the bone." Most often, that experience is from a dish that has been braised, like braised short ribs of beef, the brisket at a delicatessen, or the osso buco (braised veal shank, page 103) at an Italian restaurant. In fact, the popularity of this technique lends itself to the cooking of many cultures. If you can braise, you can make chicken cacciatore (Italy), coq au vin and *boeuf Bourguignon* (France), pork braised in soy sauce (China), and any number of other superb dishes. So braise away!

Braising is an excellent cooking method for four good reasons:

1. It is brilliant in bringing out the best in tougher and cheaper cuts of meat. When you're working with less expensive meats, which are often tougher, the effect of moisture and heat over time breaks them down to become soft and fall-off-the-bone tender.

2. In successful braising, the liquid merges with and absorbs the flavors of the other ingredients, creating an excellent sauce. The beauty of it is that it requires no extra steps to make the sauce; the braising process itself makes the sauce. When you serve a dish that has been braised, it is served in a puddle of the braising liquid.

3. It's super efficient because all the cooking is done in one pot. The classic vessel for this type of cooking is called a Dutch oven*, but one can also use either a stockpot or really any heavy-bottomed pot that's large enough to hold all the ingredients, and has a tight fitting lid.

*Don't be disgusting. Yes, I'm talking to you.

4. You get a double bonus: it's hard to screw up and the results are usually stunningly tasty.

The steps for braising are remarkably easy. Let's talk about meat. Meat is usually seared first in some hot fat to achieve the color and taste benefits of caramelization. That is known as a "brown" braise, whereas a "white" braise (i.e., no browning in advance) would more typically be used for fish or vegetables. Then, you will usually add aromatic vegetables, such as onions, garlic, carrots, and celery, after which the liquid is added. The pot is then covered and the liquid simmers over low heat for a fairly long time. I braise beef brisket (page 99), for example, for at least two hours. The cooking can be done on the stove top or in the oven, where the more even distribution of heat better prevents any burning, as long as you ensure that the liquid is simmering (i.e., meaning that it's moving gently rather than vigorously). You can be fairly sure that it will be simmering if the oven is at 350°F, but if you want to be absolutely sure you can open the oven door quickly and check.

Fish can be braised as well, but because it's more delicate than meat, it is usually done at a lower temperature and for a shorter time. You can, and should, also braise vegetables. In fact, one of my favorite dishes from cooking school was braised leeks, otherwise known by its fancy French name, *poireaux étuvés* (pwa-ROH ay-too-VAY) (see recipe on page 179). It was the first time I ever knowingly ate leeks and they were surprisingly sensational. And so simple to do. Braised in water with a dash of oil or butter and salt, they became sweet, creamy, and tender. Really delicious. Although cleaning the leeks is a slight pain in the butt—they can be dirty and sandy—it is well worth the effort. (If you want dirt in your food, eat it right from the ground.) Braised celery is also surprisingly tasty, but you can braise a lot of different veggies, from artichokes and cabbage to tomatoes and turnips, to yield exciting results.

Now remember, magnificence can't be rushed. Once you handle the simple pregame prep, which usually involves some slicing, seasoning, and searing, your ingredient becomes like a reluctant starlet who wants to be left alone—at least for a couple of hours. But that's good, too, people.

Life is fast enough; dinner shouldn't always have to be.

5. ROASTING

Unlike braising, roasting is cooking entirely with dry heat, probably the earliest cooking method. These days, food is most often roasted in the oven, but can also be done on a rotisserie or even an open flame (for you campers and cavemen). The idea is to achieve even cooking on all sides, with the primary benefit of enhanced flavor, again through the magic of caramelization. Have you ever bitten into the crispiest piece of roast chicken or pork skin? Well, those fabulous little bites of pure palate pleasure come from

proper roasting. And you now know that the by-product of the caramelization that remains in the cooking pan itself can become the basis for an extraordinary sauce.

Generally, roasting is ideal for poultry, of course, as well as more tender meats ("roasts"), potatoes and many other vegetables, such as cauliflower, squash, and Brussels sprouts. "Root vegetables," such as carrots and parsnips, are particularly good candidates for roasting because the longer cooking time fully brings out their naturally sweet flavor (caramelization again!) and softens them, too. Nuts are another category of food that benefit mightily from oven roasting. Raw nuts are really good for you; roasted nuts— cashews, almonds, peanuts, pecans, and the rest—are so delicious that they're addictive.

Roasting is usually a slower method of cooking. The term "low and slow" refers to temperature and time when roasting. The benefit of slow roasting is that there is less loss of moisture, resulting in a more tender, "juicy" product. Also, you can't really expect to roast

a big old hunk of meat too quickly, or at too high a temperature. Otherwise, you'd end up with a too crisp exterior and rawness inside. Ideally, what you're looking for in roasting is to achieve a beautiful brown, dark crust on the outside and a moist interior. In fact, it is not unusual for cooks to "sear" (that's browning by exposing to high temperature) the outside of meat first prior to placing it in the oven to cook all the way through. (Although it had been commonly believed that searing would "lock in" moisture, I must report that is simply not the case. Moisture loss is an inevitable function of heat and time.) However, searing is ideal for browning the outside and developing flavor. The objective of roasting, in any case, is to retain as much moisture as possible while developing the desired texture and color.

I recognize there are people who prefer their meat well done and many of us like the taste of char, but as I might have mentioned before, the last thing you want to end up with anything you cook is something that tastes like a dried-out shoe. Red meats such as beef and lamb are often roasted to "pink," which means it might be medium, medium rare, or even rarer. Safety dictates that you don't use this practice with poultry, which is particularly susceptible to a certain type of bacteria, so it has to reach a certain temperature to be safe.

In roasting "managing the heat" is key. You don't want to overcook or undercook. The objective is to retain as much moisture as possible with the right texture and a golden brown color. Because roasting is often done slowly over long times, it is not uncommon to baste the food with fats or liquids to maintain moisture that is naturally lost though evaporation. Roasted vegetables' readiness can often be gauged by sight; for fish, you may have to do some poking around to ensure it's cooked all the way through. However, the one surefire way to guarantee success for meat or poultry is to use a thermometer to measure internal temperature as the way to ensure it's cooked safely all the way through.

There are lots of theories about what constitutes the right temperature. My opinion is that it generally doesn't matter whether you start the oven with high temperature or low or keep it uniform throughout. What matters is ending up with moist meat and a golden brown surface at the same time. One way to achieve that is to start the oven at a very high heat and then to reduce the temperature accordingly. Another way, particularly in the case of meat, like a rack of lamb, is to "sear" or brown it before roasting it in the oven.

For equipment, all you need is a working oven and pan. (Although I have also roasted in cast-iron skillets plenty of times with particularly favorable results. It's very effective at searing and crisping skin, but since it holds in heat and will be in direct contact with ingredients, you've got to keep your eyes on the goods to ensure that don't get too crispy.) As far as recipes go, you pretty much always need to preheat your oven—that is, turning it on and getting it to the indicated temperature before you put your food in. Almost every recipe bases cooking times on a preheated oven. And since everyone's oven is different and not always calibrated to exactly the number it says on your dial, it wouldn't hurt to have an oven thermometer, or even better, to invest in an instant-read thermometer. For about fifteen bucks, this little tool will tell you instantly whether your meal is cooked perfectly or is perfectly raw inside.

Notes on heat:
- Always preheat the oven to the temperature you'll be roasting at and *have your ingredients at room temperature*.
- Know that roasted meats will continue to cook even after they're removed from the oven. This phenomenon, called "carryover cooking," is due to the residual heat from all that time in the oven.
- Let your roast rest! Please. After all that time in the hot oven, recipes should always inform you to let roasted meats and poultry sit (for anywhere from five minutes to half an hour, depending on ingredient and roasting time) in order for the juices to regenerate and resurface. If you cut into a roast too soon, you will lose most of the moist interior you're looking for. The longer it cooks, the longer you need to let it rest before carving.
- If you're roasting a large cut of beef, it's a good idea to tie it up with string before you put it in the oven. This will hold it together and promote even cooking.

- Covering. Okay, I know I said clearly that roasting is UNCOVERED, but . . . if you're roasting a turkey and the skin is starting to get a little too brown before the meat is cooked, one way to deal with that is to selectively cover the skin with aluminum foil while you continue cooking. That will allow the bird to continue cooking without ruining the skin.
- "Aromatic" vegetables, like onion, celery, and carrot, are frequently added to the roasting pan. They add flavor and moisture. Keep your eye on them, though, to ensure they don't burn.
- Broiling, under your oven's broiler, is not roasting. But it is quite effective for melty cheese, a crusty top, and a caramelized coating. Just pay attention—that is, don't leave the kitchen while you're doing it.

Oven temperature. My oven isn't "calibrated." Yours probably isn't, either. That means there is likely a difference between my 350°F and yours. And that will affect cooking times. So you have to keep your eye on food as it cooks. The point is that cooking times are always approximate. The one surefire way to guarantee that your food is cooked properly is to invest about fifteen bucks in a digital instant-read thermometer. That way, regardless of oven temperature and settings, you can poke a piece of protein to instantly ascertain its degree of doneness. If you love it medium rare, you are not going to be happy with medium well.

Meat and Poultry Roasting Chart

Meat, Type	Oven °F	Timing
BEEF, FRESH 145°F and allow to rest for at least 3 minutes.		
Beef, rib roast, bone-in; 4 to 8 pounds	325	23 to 30 min/pound
Beef, rib roast, boneless; 4 pounds	325	39 to 43 min/pound
Beef, eye round roast; 2 to 3 pounds	325	20 to 22 min/pound
Beef, tenderloin roast, whole; 4 to 6 pounds	425	45 to 60 minutes total
Beef, tenderloin roast, half; 2 to 3 pounds	425	35 to 45 minutes total
POULTRY 165°F and check the internal temperature in the innermost part of the thigh, innermost part of the wing, and the thickest part of the breast.		
Turkey, whole	325	30 min/pound
Chicken, whole; 4 to 8 pounds	375	20 to 30 min/pound
Duck, domestic, whole	375	20 min/pound
Duck, wild, whole	350	18 to 20 min/pound

LAMB 145°F and allow to rest for at least 3 minutes		
Lamb, leg, bone-in; 5 to 9 pounds	325	20 to 26 min/pound
Lamb, leg, boneless; 4 to 7 pounds	325	20 to 26 min/pound
PORK, FRESH 145°F and allow to rest for at least 3 minutes		
Pork, loin roast, bone-in; 3 to 5 pounds	325	20 to 25 min/pound
Pork, loin roast boneless; 2 to 4 pounds	325	23 to 33 min/pound
Pork, crown roast; 6 to 10 pounds	325	20 to 25 min/pound
Pork, tenderloin; ½ to 1½ pounds	425	20 to 30 minutes total
VEAL 145°F and allow to rest for at least 3 minutes		
Veal, boneless roast, rump or shoulder; 2 to 3 pounds	325	25 to 30 min/pound
Veal, bone-in roast, loin; 3 to 4 pounds	325	30 to 34 min/pound

Source: foodsafety.gov

Note: The government plays it safe, as it should. However, their suggested temperatures can lead to overcooked proteins at times. Therefore, just another reminder here that you might consider removing your meat or poultry from the heat source before it reaches the desired temperature (not eons before—but 5-10 degrees below the desired temperature will generally work). Remember that "residual" or "carryover" cooking will continue to cook the food—and raise its temperature—even after it has been taken from the heat, *especially* for those proteins that are larger and have been cooked for a longer time.

6. SAUTÉ

*Saut*é literally means *to jump* in French. In food preparation, to sauté is to move or "jump" ingredients quickly in a pan over relatively high heat with a minimal amount of fat. The idea is to brown the food while preserving its moisture. So do as Van Halen would and go ahead and jump.

When using high heat, you don't want burning, so you've got to keep the ingredients jumping. Because of the limited use of fat, it is a relatively healthy technique.

If you've ever watched a TV cooking show and have seen chefs flipping food around a pan, they're sautéing. Until you become skilled at that, you might want to use a utensil like a wooden spoon to keep the contents hopping around. Sautéing is a fast way to ease flavor out of foods that can be cooked quickly, so it is most successful when used for vegetables and thin cuts of meat or seafood that lend themselves to a quick cooking technique. Thinly sliced chicken breast, shrimp, onions, and mushrooms are all good examples. The ideal result is that you will caramelize the outer surface of what you're sautéing and simultaneously cook the inside sufficiently as well. In other words, you'll be looking for a little browning.

Sautéing is different from panfrying. In a sauté, the pieces of food are kept small and cooked quickly. Panfrying is done with larger ingredients (think pork chops) and cooked thoroughly on one side before being turned over to cook the other. Sautéing is not the same as searing either. Remember that in searing, you're only cooking the surface of the food to brown it effectively. The cooking method that is closest to sautéing is stir-frying. The primary difference is that stir-frying is an ancient Chinese method, usually done using a wok. They both use high heat and a little lubrication to cook small-sized ingredients quickly.

The wok's rounded pan facilitates the perpetual motion of the ingredients. Somewhat like a sauté, "sweating" is the term used to describe the technique of cooking aromatic vegetables over low heat in a little fat so as to soften them without letting them brown. It is often a preliminary step to making soups, sauces, and braises.

The five basic rules of sautéing:

1. Use a very hot pan. Remember, this is a quick cooking method.

2. Lubricate LIGHTLY with fat. You'll need lubrication even if you are using a nonstick skillet. You generally use fat of some sort, most commonly oil or butter, but not too much of it. This is not frying and you don't want greasy; you're looking for brown and crisp, not leaden.

3. Make sure your ingredients are dry. Otherwise too much liquid accumulates in the pan and again leads to soggy. The idea in sautéing is to eliminate some of the natural "water" from the ingredients; in this case, their water content is barrier to full flavor.

4. Do not crowd the pan. Overcrowding in our schools is a problem; same in our sauté pans. Ingredients need direct access to the heat from the bottom of the pan. More than one layer of food in the pan and you get mush.

5. Do not cover the pan. The effect of covering is to steam, which leads to soggy. That is the opposite of what we're looking for, which is crisp.

Utensils: For most sautés, your average, everyday frying pan will do. Or a skillet, or what they call a sauté pan. Although skillets with flat sides rather than rounded ones will keep more food inside the pan—rather than jumping out of it—pans with rounded sides, like woks, which are shaped like big bowls, facilitate the perpetual motion of the ingredients. Remember, if it's not jumping, you're not really sautéing.

If you want to practice: Different foods with different textures have different cooking times. However, in performing a sauté all the ingredients are thrown in the pan at once and they're cooked quickly. Your sauté pan must be large enough to hold all of the food in one layer. The food has to be in direct contact with the heat underneath it and in direct contact with the air above it; it can't be covered by other food or a lid. That's because we don't want our sauté to be a failure, which it will be if we steam and stew the food rather than brown it.

Because we're cooking quickly over high heat, you must keep moving the ingredients frequently, either by moving them around rapidly with a spatula or, by jerking the pan repeatedly to make the ingredients "jump." The sauté technique involves gripping the handle of the sauté pan firmly, and using a sharp elbow motion to rapidly jerk the pan back toward the cook, repeating as necessary to insure that the ingredients have been thoroughly jumped. This is what you always see the TV chefs do, and with a little practice, you will be doing it yourself in no time. Although, in the beginning, expect that there will be food flying everywhere.

"The sauté is a method that should come most naturally to men because it requires repeated jerking."

CLARIFIED BUTTER

Clarified butter is what you get when you remove the "milk solids" and water from regular butter. When those milk solids and water are (easily) removed, you are left with pure butterfat. The advantage of this clarified butter, especially as it pertains to sautéing, is that it can be used at a much higher temperature without burning or browning. Regular butter will burn at high heat because of those milk solids, whereas clarified butter has a much higher "smoke point."

How to clarify butter: You certainly don't need to, but it's easier than it might sound. Melt butter slowly over low heat and let it sit for a few minutes. No stirring. Then skim and discard all that white foam off the top and carefully pour the liquefied butterfat into a dish or container, leaving behind the "milky solids" in the bottom of the pan. (You could also strain the melted butter through cheese cloth or a coffee filter—I've even used a paper towel.) You want to end up with just pure golden liquid, no white bits. And by the way, it's always better to cook with unsalted butter so that YOU can control the dish's salt level. Incidentally, you can also buy ghee, the clarified butter used in Indian cooking.

7. SEASONING

In general, seasoning is the process of using salt, pepper, herbs, and spices to give flavor to food. It should be pointed out that that the strictest definition of seasoning refers only to the addition of salt to a preparation. However, for the purposes of us home cooks, we'll cover the whole category. When it comes to herbs and spices, recipes will specify amounts, but you will also notice that many recipes include the instruction to "taste and adjust for seasoning as necessary." That seasoning refers to salt and pepper, an amount that varies by person depending on their taste.

So this is a good moment to mention that no seasoning is more important than salt. More than any other seasoning in the world, salt is what brings out flavor in food. Most savory food, like meats or poultry, would have relatively no taste without salt. Why? There is nothing in the ingredient inherently that would trigger any of your taste buds, which are responsive only to sweet, bitter, sour, or salt. This should come as no surprise to anyone who has ever eaten. Just read the ingredients on food labels and you will see salt in almost everything, even foods you don't think of as savory, such as desserts. Most cakes,

cookies, brownies, cereals, etc. have salt in them for the same reason mentioned earlier—it brings out flavor in food. However, we Americans tend to go a little overboard on just about everything, and that includes salt, which causes high blood pressure. Consequently, salt overuse can actually become somewhat of a health hazard. Anyone who has a condition that will limit their salt intake will probably have to use salt substitutes and can also compensate by using herbs and spices; but as a cook, I have to admit that real salt is virtually irreplaceable in terms of its impact on food's flavor.

UMAMI

What is it that makes some foods taste really, really good? It could be umami, the "fifth taste."

All of our lives we've been told that the tongue can discern four different tastes. Well it turns out all these years later that there's a fifth taste your tongue can identify. It's called umami. It's almost like being told that Pluto is no longer a planet. Anyway, umami is actually a "savory" sensation. What's savory? It's that rich, deep flavor you get in your mouth from foods like cheese, and steak with mushrooms. You know that big explosion of flavor you get in your mouth when you take a bite of blue cheese? That's because it's an umami rich food. As is meat. As are oysters. And sautéed mushrooms, for example. All foods rich with umami.

Now, you may not have heard of umami before, but I can assure you that chefs have. That's why when you go to a restaurant you often have a meal that leaves you wondering why you can't cook like that at home. It's because they know how to maximize the umami—or the taste quotient—of what you're eating. But if you want to add some extra umami flavor to your cooking at home, it's not that hard to do. When you make a vegetable soup, for example, add in a whole handful of shiitake or porcini mushrooms. When you're making a sauce, it's a good idea to put in some tomato paste because it adds a depth and richness of flavor. And any time you add soy sauce or Worcestershire sauce to a preparation, you're bringing an element of umami to your meal.

If you don't feel like cooking, then go out to a steak restaurant for an umami blast. Ever wonder why people are having such a good time at a steak house joint? Look at the menu. You start off with a shrimp cocktail, followed by a Caesar salad with anchovies and cheese in it. And a beautiful piece of steak with mushroom sauce. All umami-rich foods!

(Plus, that goblet of Cabernet doesn't hurt either.)

Now that we've touched on salt, it's time to talk about some of the most important herbs and spices. First, herbs are aromatic plants. Parsley, sage, rosemary, and thyme is more than just a song lyric; they are some of the most common herbs.

Herbs can be used either fresh or dried, depending on availability and recipe. They are mostly interchangeable in cooking—recipes tend to suggest use dried herbs in dishes that cook for a long time—but I could NEVER imagine a platter of beautiful tomatoes, served with a fresh mozzarella and drizzled with fragrant olive (with a pinch of salt of course) that was topped by sprinkle of dried basil instead of fresh. That just doesn't fly. The point is that there is an ideal use for both; fresh herbs are usually preferred when consuming fresh food or for preparations that do not require long cooking, such as braising and roasting, when dried herbs serve the purpose well.

Like herbs, spices are also the aromatic by-product of plants. The primary difference is that spices are usually sold in seed or powder form and they are quite fragrant, or sharp flavored. The most widely use spices are pepper(corns), cinnamon, ginger, nutmeg, bay leaves, cumin, and chile. Certain dishes are unimaginable (impossible, actually) without spices. It wouldn't be much of a chili without chili powder or a very tasty gingerbread cookie without ginger. Entire cuisines are dependent on certain herbs and spices. What would a Chinese meal taste like without ginger, scallion, and garlic? Indian food without curry powder, Hungarian food without paprika? I don't think so. Indeed, apart from salt, herbs and spices are what bring maximum flavor and pleasure to all that we eat.

"Variety's the very spice of life that gives it all its flavor."
—William Cowper

When Flavors Collide

As a general rule, certain herbs and spices pair well with certain foods. As a second general rule, certain herbs and spices clash with certain foods *and* with each other. I'll never forget roasting a chicken in cooking school that I flavored with rosemary and tarragon. A no-no, apparently. My teacher tasted it and instantly pointed out that the rosemary, an *herb de Provence*, did not belong together with the tarragon, one of the *fines herbes*. (I told you French cooking is disciplined.)

In baking, it is common to see cinnamon and nutmeg used together, and sometimes allspice and clove, too. The so-called *herbes de Provence* (thyme, rosemary, basil, bay, savory) are commonly combined in French food. Oregano, marjoram, and basil are big in Italian and Greek cookery. Then you have the intensely aromatic flavors of cumin, coriander, and cardamom.

Their lively flavors wake up recipes from other parts of the world, but trust me when I tell you that they would not go well with dishes whose flavor profile is distinctly Italian, French, or American influenced. Or don't trust me and judge for yourself.

In the beginning, you should follow recipes as they are intended, but over time and with a little more experience in the kitchen, I would encourage you to improvise and try new things. Just remember that when it comes to experimenting with herbs and spices, some work very well together and some don't. Knowing how to season, what to season with, and what seasonings go best with what foods will make you a far better cook. And it's not too hard to learn.

Three Herbs and Spices That Will Instantly Improve Your Cooking

It is amazing how easy it can be to add a lot of flavor to food. That may sound obvious, but we often eat the very same food, prepared the very same way, over and over again. Yet, with the simple shake of a little glass jar, you can bring an entirely new and exciting taste dimension to your meals.

Here are three readily available herbs and spices that I use frequently to totally titillate my taste buds.

1. **Ancho Chile Powder.** The word "chile" does not necessarily translate into "spicy." Of course there are chilies that will blow your doors off, but there are also those that are mild, and others that are even considered kind of "fruity." The ancho chile is one of those, not hot, but with a mellow hint of raisin. You can buy and cook them whole, but I suggest you use the already ground powder. (Available in many supermarkets.) You'll have to decide for yourself, but to me it brings an earthy, fragrant New Mexican accent to foods. Sprinkle it on chicken pieces before roasting or season raw shrimp with it (and salt) and then sauté in a little olive oil with sliced garlic, finishing it with a squeeze of lime and fresh chopped cilantro. Nothing wrong with that. Not only delicious, the powder adds an appetizing rust color to your dish.

2. **Smoked Spanish Paprika.** Also called *pimentón*, it's very much in vogue these days among the foodies, which is understandable because it's the simplest way conceivable to bring a rich, smoky (Spanish) flavor profile to your palate. You could use it in so many ways, adding it to whatever might be enhanced by its smokiness, such as meats, potatoes, eggs, and dressings. I pour it over a batch of chickpeas, out of the can and rinsed. I add olive oil and salt and toss 'em into the toaster oven at 425 for just long enough to get it slightly crisp on the outside, but still soft and chewy inside, about 10–12 minutes. These things disappear before dinner and, for what it's worth, I hear they're good for you, too.

3. *Herbes de Provence.* Don't let the fancy French name fool you; you can buy a bottle of it at most supermarkets, and the stuff rocks. Why? Because Provence is in the southwest of France, home to some of the most delicious food in the entire world, mainly due to its locally grown ingredients. In the case of herbs, that translates into rosemary, fennel, thyme, savory, basil, lavender, chervil, and marjoram. It's fantastic, actually, because rather than having to measure and shake out eight different bottles into your recipe, you can have it properly blended and ready to go from just one. How to use? We love its flavor on roast chicken, potatoes, and added into the morning eggs. Use it on fish and vegetables, to fancify your vinaigrette, or on anything you wish to grace with a breath of the French countryside. I think you'll be happy.

Other Seasoning

There are other "seasonings" aside from the saline (salty) ones. And there are many ways to incorporate their varied flavors and accents into cooking. There are the acids (vinegar and citrus, for example), hot seasoning (peppers, peppercorns, and the likes), and saccharine seasonings (such as sugar and honey, common in baking). There are also plenty of condiments, from mustards and horseradish to ketchup and Worcestershire, and flavorful fats (infused oils) that you will use to excite your palate.

8. BOILING, BLANCHING, and POACHING

These three methods all involve cooking that uses the action of liquid, most often water. They all require that ingredients are submerged in the water. The difference between the three is the intensity of the boil and the duration of the cooking. Boiling, as we remember from grade school, is when fresh water (at sea level) is heated to 212 degrees. When it becomes very vigorous, cooks call it a rolling boil. When very gently bubbling, it is referred to as simmering. Blanching is the use of boiling water to prepare foods, usually vegetables, often before cooking them further by another method. Blanching is a quick process; you're not looking to cook something to death, but rather to remove its firm rawness, and in the case of green vegetables in particular, to maintain its vibrant greenness (which actually requires that you place your blanched veggies into a bowl of ice water in a process called "shocking"). For instance, you might briefly blanch broccoli to soften it before sautéing it olive oil. Poaching is the process of gently cooking food in simmering liquid (whether water, stock, milk, wine, etc.) For example, you might poach pears in water and sugar (or red wine) to make a simple, sweet dessert (see page 213).

Boiling can be used to cook most anything. It is a particularly efficient way to cook firm or hearty food such as meats, potatoes, shrimp, chicken, vegetables, beans, and even peanuts. And of course, there's no other way to cook pasta. The challenge with cooking in boiling water is that you can overdo it, in which case you end up with limp, soggy, and tasteless. You can boil the taste right out of food and destroy its texture. Pasta, for example, is ideal when al dente, meaning that it still has a little bit of a chew to it. No one really wants noodles that are slimy and gummy.

Poaching, on the other hand, is a delicate cooking method, which is why it is most commonly associated with eggs and salmon. If you tried cooking soft-fleshed fish in boiling water, it would disintegrate. But when you're looking for that perfect runny yellow yoke for your eggs benny, poaching is the way to play. And if you're really feeling decadent (or very thin, or very rich) you can even poach in butter or olive oil.

Court-Bouillon

In cooking school, they call it a *Court-Bouillon* (core-boo-yone). To me, it's basically highly flavored water that you'd use to poach fish or vegetables. It's an effective way to bring fresh flavor to light food. You'd simply infuse water with some combination of aromatics (garlic, onion, etc.), herbs, and perhaps wine or vinegar. Boil and reduce to a simmer and you've got yourself a tasty broth to cook with.

The beauty of blanching is that it's simple, fast, and effective. Try it with some nice fresh string beans: place them in a well-salted pot of boiling water until they soften a little, but still maintain some crunchiness. Immediately strain them into a bowl filled with water and ice. By shocking them, you will notice that their color stays a vibrant green. Now, go ahead and give them a quick sauté in butter or in olive oil, drop in a handful of sliced almonds, and you've just made string beans almondine. But if you want to get lucky, call it by its fancy French name, *haricots verts aux amandes*.

What about steaming? Another way to cook with boiling liquid, but the food is not actually submerged in it. But be very careful: steam can be as hot as boiling water.

9. FRYING

Frying is, quite simply, cooking food in oil or fat. It is one of the oldest cooking methods known to man. Although almost every culture has its version of fabulous fried food—tempura in Japan, fish and chips in England, schnitzel in Germany, Italy's *fritto misto*, Israeli falafel—America is the reigning Super Bowl champion

of frying. And with good reason: it's what makes everything from French fries to fried chicken taste so damn good! When you consider the popularity of the frying method, it even transcends meat and potatoes and goes right into dessert as well. Beignets in New Orleans, zeppoles and funnel cakes at street and county fairs, and doughnuts sold on almost every main street in America are, of course, all versions of deep-fried dough.

There are various forms of frying, of which deep-frying and panfrying are the most widely used. Frying methods basically differ based on the amount of fat required as well as the vessel in which the food is fried. Whichever the method, cooking in very hot fat produces both an amazing taste and texture. Frying is not the easiest technique to master due to the number of variables involved—i.e., types of fats, different methods, and cooking times. However, when done well, frying gives you everything you want from food. It gives you the taste (from caramelization) and it gives you the texture, that is, crispy on the outside, yet soft and fluffy on the inside in the case of

a doughnut, or juicy on the inside in the case of fried chicken. (I suppose you could also add gooey inside in the case of the deep-fried Three Musketeers bar.) Frying is why we love foods like French fries, clams, shrimp, onion rings, Chinese egg rolls, calamari, green tomatoes, and hush puppies so much. Oh, and don't forget potato chips and tortilla chips, too!

Deep-frying is exactly what it sounds like—ingredients are totally immersed in hot oil. Think French fries at Mickey D's. Obviously this method uses the most oil because the food is completely surrounded by it. It is an ideal method to cook potatoes, chicken, and foods that are "battered" or "breaded," like seafood (clams and shrimp) and vegetables (eggplant or artichokes). When deep-frying is done right, you end up with crispness, of course, not soggy and leaden from oil. Panfrying is different because you use enough oil to cover about a third to half of the ingredient you're cooking. With this method, you cook one side of an item first, usually in some type of frying pan, and then it's turned over to cook on the other side. Panfrying is ideal for ingredients like pork chops and certain fish because it leads to really nice browning of the food. Stir-frying is a third frying method worth mentioning just briefly. It is a useful technique that's actually very similar to sautéing, but based on Chinese wok cooking, which employs a rounded pan to stir and toss finely chopped food over high heat for quick cooking. It uses just enough oil to provide sufficient lubrication and it requires that the ingredients are moved around continuously around the pan. That's what a wok was built for, to facilitate the perpetual motion of ingredients over high heat to get them just cooked and crisp. When you think of Chinese food, you can understand how stir-frying would be effective for anything from thinly sliced proteins like meat, chicken, and seafood to vegetables and even (fried) rice.

Because all frying methods employ fats in varying amounts, let's cover some of the basics about fats. As you know, there are many different types of oils, such as olive, vegetable, corn, peanut, canola, and safflower, to name just a few. Different oils impart different flavors and have different smoke points, which

simply means they smoke up at different temperatures. Therefore, certain oils are better for certain uses. Whereas olive oil might be fine for light sautéing or low heat cooking, peanut oil, vegetable oil, and sunflower oil are better for high-heat frying. Also, olive oil adds a lot of flavor to foods, so it

How to Tell When Oil Is Hot Enough to Fry

If you don't have a thermometer designed specifically for oil, here are three tricks to see if the oil is at the right temperature to fry:

1. Place the handle of a wooden spoon, or a chopstick, into the oil and watch for bubbles to collect around it.
2. Drop an unpopped popcorn kernel into the oil. It will pop when the oil is at the right temperature to deep-fry.
3. Put a cube of bread in the oil. When it sizzles, it's ready.

would be wonderful when frying artichokes, for example. Canola oil, on the other hand, is neutral, and is preferred when the item being fried would not benefit from the taste of the oil, such as doughnuts. As mentioned before, you can also fry in "clarified" butter (see sidebar on Clarified Butter) and lard (animal fat), which produces some great taste and texture, but is generally frowned upon for reasons of health.

What about health? You've all heard about good oil and bad oil. Hydrogenated oil clogs the arteries, so you want to avoid those. Oils such as olive oil, canola, and other plant-based oils are said to be heart healthier. A lot has been said about horrors of frying food and in this country, and we do have the tendency to overdo it. But that doesn't mean we can't enjoy French fries every once in a while. Unless you want to die young I wouldn't advocate deep-frying at every meal. But I certainly wouldn't advocate avoiding it altogether because it also adds immeasurably to quality of life. I mean, what's life without French fries? Or fried chicken? Or doughnuts?

So go ahead and fry, baby, fry! In moderation.

10. BAKING

They taught us baking in cooking school. I don't remember getting a particularly good grade. Because I didn't. Although I prefer the intuitive nature, spontaneity, and the flames that constitute savory cooking, I can also attest to the fact that baking is a beautiful thing. So if you get into cooking, you might find yourself interested in baking, too. I'm pretty positive that fresh baked cookies are superior to store-bought. (Although I'm not as certain they're always as good as bakery bought.)

Compared to cooking, baking is a totally different animal. (Well, actually, there's no animal involved at all, unless you count animal crackers or elephant ears.) Why? Because baking is very much about science. Specifically, chemistry. As such, one aspect that sets it apart is specificity. Whereas most of the recipes I present here leave room for improvisation, variation, and seasoning options, baking is characterized by more exact measurements and timing. I mean that breads and cakes don't rise to the occasion, literally, if you haven't used the precise ingredients, measurements, and proportions called for by a recipe. I would also contend that for the most part, not only is baking more methodical and disciplined, it is generally more time-consuming and leaves more to clean up. As you might realize by now, those are not a few of my favorite things. But they do lend themselves to a lovely weekend activity. And baking is great to do with kids.

Baking also requires an entirely different set of skills, techniques, tools, and ingredients.

As for tools, among some others, you'd probably want to have baking pans, electric mixers, mixing bowls, a rolling pin, and a pastry brush available. (Of course you'll need measuring cups and spoons, but you should have those anyway.) Some of the more common ingredients you'll find listed in baking recipes include eggs and extracts, various baking flours and powders, alternative sweeteners and fats. The array of spices you would likely encounter include allspice, cardamom, cinnamon, cloves, ginger, and nutmeg. And don't forget a whole mess of chocolate, I hope.

Even the terminology used in baking is different. Perhaps even a little kinky. I'm not referring to weighing, sifting, folding, and decorating. Baking is filled with words that seem to run the gamut from sexy to downright dangerous. Greasing. Kneading. Melting. Piping. Whipping. And Creaming. I can't tell if they're making a cake or a porn movie.

> I can't tell if they're making a cake or a porn movie.

Although it's not my preferred technique, I know some dudes who love it. There is no question that baking your own bread from scratch and watching it transform into a piping hot, crusty, chewy loaf of goodness is not only a thrill, it is really good eating. And you might already know how gratifying it is to call those brownies you make for the bake sale "homemade." Just because I'm not as turned on by parchment paper, pastry bags, and pie weights as I am by fire, filets, and frankfurters, doesn't mean you might not be. In fact, in the chapter on Sweet Things you'll find a few of the simple items I bake and that you might want to attempt as well.

CHAPTER FIVE

THE THING ABOUT RECIPES (AND HOW TO LOOK AT THEM)

One of the first things you learn when you cook for a while is that recipes are necessary and important, yet not always perfect or flawless. Nor will they all be to your liking, either. Our taste buds are different. What one person finds too salty, another may perceive as not seasoned enough. Naturally, the same goes for too oily, too spicy, and too anything, for that matter. That comes with the territory.

Judy Rodgers was an influential American chef who was quoted as saying, "Recipes do not make food taste good, people do." It's true that two people can follow the exact same recipe in the same way and end up with completely different results. It's also the case that the quality of the ingredients you begin with have a significant impact on the final product. Fresher produce will almost always be superior to canned. Better meat makes a better burger. Higher quality oil matters. And so on. That holds true for almost any ingredient at all. Which is why I've always advocated . . .

Get the best ingredients you can . . . and don't mess 'em up too much.

That experience of writing this book was invaluable because it reminded me how much I like making food and feeding my people. And eating what I've made. There is not one recipe included that I wouldn't be happy to cook again. It also served as a reminder of the inherent limitations of recipes. Recipes are guides, not unlike maps. They provide directions to a destination—however, that doesn't mean it's the only way to get there. Even your GPS gives you options. As you follow the directions and ingredient list I provide here, remember that nothing is more important than how something tastes to you and the people you're cooking for. Which is why it's so important, whenever possible, to *taste what you're making at each step of the process along the way*. It's why most recipes, from time immemorial, always include some version of the words "taste for seasoning" and directions to "adjust to taste" accordingly.

The process of writing this book also recalled something I was taught in cooking school by my excellent teacher, James Peterson, who himself went on to write extraordinary cookbooks, including *Sauces*, considered to be the "bible" on the subject. He taught that you read through a recipe to glean basic information. What will the cooking method be? A sauté, a braise, or a roast, for example. How much time will be involved? To shop for it, to prep, to cook. And of course, what are the key ingredients? To that he added the question of what, if any, substitutions or alterations we'd be making. The recipe was a starting point, but no savory recipe was necessarily considered to be entirely set in stone. There is usually some room for adjustment, refinement, and/or adaptation. Admittedly, there are certain recipes that do require a stricter adherence to the formula, especially when it comes to the more precise measurements and specific ingredients used in baking.

There are other considerations that affect recipe results. My oven is likely calibrated at a different temperature from yours. My pans might not distribute the heat from a flame the same way yours do. Or we have a different perception of what "medium high" heat looks like. Especially if you're using electric and I have a gas flame. Or we're cooking at different altitudes. Or rather than being at room temperature, maybe your leg of lamb was still quite cold on the inside when you put it in the oven. Any of which means that foods might not cook for exactly the same amount of time indicated. That's why you see estimated cooking times in recipes.

When it comes to measurements, my *large lemon* might release a whole lot more juice than your little one. Or my *medium onion* may not be the same size as yours. And just what constitutes a "handful," especially if our hands are different sizes? In these cases, I'll always try to include a measurement that does the job (e.g., 1 teaspoon lemon juice, ¼ cup onion) for the sake of clarity and consistency. But as you can see, there is often some wiggle room.

You should also understand the role of substitutions. If you, your family, or your friends absolutely detest cilantro, for example, simply remove it from a recipe. Better yet, as herbs are generally interchangeable, replace it with another fresh herb you prefer. If you're sensitive to salt, use less than what's called for, and consider readily available salt substitutes. You're not a garlic lover? Don't sweat it. Use onion, shallot, or leek instead.

What about the number of servings? Recipes usually indicate how many portions they make. That would be fine if there was one standard serving size for every type of food that we all agreed upon. But I'm guessing that my dainty daughters don't consume the same humongous portions as your sons who play on the varsity football squad. So that rack of ribs that I suggest serves two could probably serve one very hungry eater. Or feed four folks if presented as an appetizer instead.

Recipes are your road map. Over time, and with a little experience, you will become an expert navigator. Most recipes are somewhat forgiving and flexibility is fine. So if something tastes better to you a certain way, go for it. As I said from the beginning, the idea is for you to find the dishes that you can not only master, but even go ahead and make your own. And unless you're being paid to make the meal, don't be afraid to make mistakes.

No Stylists Were Harmed In The Making Of This Book

To prepare for the book's photography, I made all one

hundred recipes over nine days. I had no help in the kitchen. I did all the cutting, chopping, cooking, and plating myself. So . . . no stylists were harmed in the making of this book. To be fair, however, my ace photographer Josephine Rozman (Jo Ro) has both a great eye and a wonderful aesthetic, so I'm sure the plates you see pictured here do look better than they would if you came over to my place for dinner on an average evening. Jo and I decided on how to best present the food—using my own plates, by the way—and all the photos were shot in my living room, using only natural light. Even though I've never been big on "plating," as they call it (I'm much more about the taste than the look of the food), I did it this way not only to be cost-efficient (i.e., cheap), but so that readers could see what these dishes should look like without relying on experts, stylists, studio lighting, and retouching to make them look perfect.

A Note on Intuitive Cooking

Note to my fellow males: It has long been a historical generalization or perhaps a truism than men don't like maps or following directions. Although that might not be true, it is true for me. Which is to say that I will glance at a recipe to get a basic idea of what's required, then I'll go off and make it my own way. Indeed, much of what I make these days is what I call "intuitive" cooking. By that I mean that I might survey a recipe, see a concept I like, and apply those principles to ingredients I already have on hand or those that look good at the market on that day. Intuitive cooking also applies to making substitutions in recipes. So if you're making biscotti with a recipe that calls for dried cherries (page 225) then of course you can use other dried fruit in its place. Unless almonds, for example, are absolutely mandatory to a recipe's final result, feel free to substitute other nuts with a similar (hard) texture. You'll see a few recipes here marked **"intuitive"** that are especially good and easy to adapt. That's my way of inviting you to use your intuition.

Since I'm very big on taking advantage of whatever leftovers I have on hand, intuitive cooking comes into play regularly. My eggs puttanesca (page 63) is a creation based on the Italian pasta dish of the same name, but adapted instead for breakfast. My oatmeal brûlée (page 71) was born out of that delicious crack of caramelized sugar atop the classic French dessert crème brûlée. I'll admit that intuitive cooking comes more naturally once you've had more experience in the kitchen. Therein lies the intention behind this book. Take what I've learned, practice it yourself, and feel free to use your own intuition as you see fit. Let the recipes serve as a guide, of course. But once you're comfortable with some of the basics, have at it. Worst case is that you'll mess it up, learn how not to do it, and order that pizza instead.

P.S. Just try not to experiment too much when using expensive ingredients. Remember . . .

"Mess up oatmeal, not veal."

Salt. All recipes included here assume kosher salt. Not only is it easier to apply by hand, but iodized table salt can have a slightly bitter taste. That's why many chefs cook with coarse kosher salt rather than table salt. For a few bucks a box, you should too. Kosher salt grains are larger than table salt, so be aware that measurements have to be adjusted if you use table salt. (Use less volume indicated in the recipe.) Of course, if you're sensitive to salt, use less. You can always add. And remember to season at each stage of the cooking process, rather than just at the end.

Oil. You will find many recipes that call for oil, sometimes to cook with, other times to add atop a finished dish. Here's a general rule I follow: When the oil is a key component of a dish, by all means, use the best quality olive oil you can. For cooking with oil, as mentioned previously, olive is fine for quick sautés, whereas the neutral oils are better for high heat cooking and frying.

Herbs and spices. Some people despise cumin, others can't tolerate garlic. Cilantro is another of those polarizing herbs that certain folks hate. So by all means skip it—*not the recipe*—and use parsley or some other herb instead. Disliking a single ingredient doesn't preclude you from making that dish. (Although I'd argue that guacamole without cilantro is not guacamole.) Naturally, this holds true for any herbs or spices you simply can't stand. There is always an alternative.

Keeping It Clean

Chefs know that it's easy to add taste appeal by using plenty of fat and salt. Most of my recipes try to be conscious about calories. There is no deep-frying; there's not too much cream, mayo, or butter. I try not to use too much salt or sugar. I'm not being preachy. I'm not advocating for the abstemious. I'm merely exercising some restraint so as to minimize unnecessary caloric intake while still ensuring the food tastes great.

The Taste-to-Effort Equation

The most taste with the fewest ingredients and the least effort ™. It all starts with the recipe, which indicates how many ingredients you'll need, how many steps it will take, how much time you'll need, and the overall degree of difficulty involved. In fact, I've developed my own kind of internal measuring system. It's somewhat imprecise, but the idea is clear: some dishes are worth the effort, others are simply not. Here's an example: littleneck clams on the grill. You throw some clams on the grill, close the lid, and when the clams open—having steamed in their own salty juices—they are ready to eat. Voilà! And I've had people ask me for the recipe. Quite simply, perhaps one of the greatest single-ingredient dishes in the world . . . unless firing up a grill is considered too much effort.

The Taste-to-Effort Equation

Low effort, Big Taste

Totally worth it

Lotta effort, Big Taste

Not worth it
(unless someone else is making it)

When I see a recipe with so many ingredients my eyes start to glaze over, I lose interest. That said, there are some recipes with only a few ingredients that can still be complicated to prepare. One such I've included here is the Serious Chocolate Cake (page 232). Melting chocolate is easy, but whipping eggs over heat until they reach the right thickness is a technique that requires a certain level of knowhow and patience. Then there's folding, greasing, water baths . . . etc. Doable, but not necessarily simple. The result, however, is an intense and decadent chocolate cake, made without flour, that I think *is* worth doing.

I hope it's obvious that I've only included recipes that are worth the effort. I've seen plenty of recipes that I'd never bother making. Not because I don't like the dish. But because, why bother? Like mango chutney. Too many ingredients. Too complicated. Too much time. And perfectly excellent from that jar in the supermarket. That is not the case with tomato sauce or vinaigrette, both of which I urge you to make rather than purchase.

RESULTS MAY VARY

Never have truer words been spoken, particularly when it comes to recipes. One of the things you learn from experience along the way is that two people may follow the same recipe in the same way, using the same specifications called for, and end up with different results. And not due to their level of skill, either, but to some of the factors I mentioned earlier. But mostly the ingredients themselves. Brilliant local tomatoes from a farm stand at their peak of perfect ripeness will beat off-season store-bought ones all the time, especially for recipes where tomatoes are a central ingredient. Remember, the recipe is your starting point and most helpful guide. You will get the optimal results by using ingredients when they're at their best.

Now, let's cook!

CHAPTER SIX

WAKE UP, IT'S A BEAUTIFUL MORNING

We direct much psychic and physical energy toward dinner (the accepted de facto dining ritual, portrayed by conventional wisdom as the ideal time to dissect the day over protein, a starch, and a vegetable). But in the thick of the morning rush, we often treat breakfast as a mere nutritional necessity. However, elevating breakfast doesn't have to be complicated or time-consuming.

AVOCADO TOAST

This has become increasingly popular everywhere you look, and with good reason. Avocado is nutritious, creamy, and delicious. Kids and grownups alike love it, whether in guacamole or, in this case, on a slice of toast. The key is to get a nice ripe avocado, one that yields a bit to the touch when you apply pressure to it. You can keep it simple with just a sprinkle of salt, or add pistachios, a slice of tomato, red pepper flakes if you like a little spice, a slice of turkey or prosciutto for added protein, or anything else that delights you. Whatever you do, don't tell the kids it's loaded with health.

MAKES 2–3 TOASTS

INGREDIENTS
1 RIPE AVOCADO*
2–3 SLICES TOASTED BREAD
SALT TO TASTE

OPTIONAL TOPPINGS: TOASTED NUTS, SLICE OF TOMATO, PROSCIUTTO, RED PEPPER FLAKES, SLICE OF TURKEY, AN EGG . . . ETC.

About the ripe avocado, there is a joke that goes like this . . .
Not yet
Not yet
Not yet
Not yet
Not yet
EAT ME NOW
Too late.
—Avocados

* It should yield slightly to pressure, but can't be too soft. If that's good, then pop off that little stem at the top. You're looking for a greenish yellow, NOT brown.

PREPARATION

1. Halve the avocado lengthwise, remove the pit, and scoop it out.

2. Slice and mash onto hot toast.

3. Sprinkle with salt . . . and whatever else!

Photo by Robert Rosenthal

BREAKFAST PIZZA

Breakfast can be routine and boring. So . . . why not pizza for a change? It's bread and cheese with a touch of tomato sauce. Although you could use any toasted bread, I make them on a flour tortilla and finish them right in the toaster oven. Crispy, melty, tasty goodness that's mighty easy to prepare. They're excellent on bagels too, which are good to make ahead and freeze.

INGREDIENTS

1 8-INCH FLOUR TORTILLA

1–2 TABLESPOONS TOMATO SAUCE (SEE PAGE 149 OR BOTTLED)

1 HANDFUL SHREDDED CHEESE

PREPARATION

1. Top the tortilla with tomato sauce and cheese.

2. Toast or bake until tortilla is crispy and cheese has melted.

3. Slice and serve to cute kids.

SUPER BREAKFAST BURRITO (INTUITIVE)

I just inhaled one myself. Extremely appetizing and satisfying, it's essentially scrambled eggs mixed with a few other zesty ingredients wrapped inside a soft flour tortilla. Cheese seems like a must, maybe a few veggies, and perhaps a breakfast meat. No one wants to spend a ton of time cooking in the morning, so the trick is to use what's on hand and pretty much ready to go without a lot of prep. For example, already shredded or sliced cheese is an obvious time-saver. Nothing wrong with last night's leftovers, chopped up, whether vegetables, potatoes, or whatever. This is all about variations; you decide what makes it "super" in yours. That soft tortilla filled with a splendid mélange of your favorite breakfast foods is a great way to start the day and a delight to eat.

Note: I like to "toast" the tortilla for a few seconds over an open flame to add a little blast of char to taste, but it's not at all necessary.

Something just occurred to me: If you happen to have any salami on hand, you might chop and toss some right into the hot pan as your starting point. There was a famous old Catskills comedian by the name of Alan King who co-wrote a book entitled, *Is Salami and Eggs Better Than Sex?* Just thought you should know.

MAKES 1

INGREDIENTS

ENOUGH OIL OR BUTTER TO LUBRICATE PAN (ABOUT
1½ TEASPOONS)
OPTIONS INCLUDE . . . 1 TABLESPOON OR SO OF ANY
OF THE FOLLOWING, CHOPPED:
ONION OR SCALLION, GREEN OR RED BELL
PEPPER, TOMATO
1 PIECE OF BACON OR SERVING OF BREAKFAST
SAUSAGE, HAM, OR TURKEY
2 EGGS, BEATEN
1 HANDFUL OF GRATED CHEESE OR 1 SLICE OF
CHEDDAR OR AMERICAN
1 8-INCH FLOUR TORTILLA

PREPARATION

1. Drizzle oil into pan over medium high heat and sauté whatever vegetables you use together with any meats until all cooked through.

2. Scramble in eggs and cheese to the desired level of doneness.

3. Place and fold inside tortilla, slice in half, and say good morning to deliciousness. Hot sauce is, of course, always an option.

EGGS PUTTANESCA

This dish is inspired by the famed Italian *spaghetti alla puttanesca*, which, to be frank, translates into *whore-style spaghetti*. Long story. You might not want to mention that to the kids, either. In any case, it's a way of bringing a ton of flavor—AND any leftover pasta from the night before—to the morning's eggs. I've eliminated the garlic and anchovies that would normally go into the pasta version; this is breakfast, after all. But you won't miss them. It's that good. As always, feel free to throw in whatever other sensible scraps you might find in the fridge—that is the very nature of this whore's dish.

SERVES 2

INGREDIENTS
1 TABLESPOON OLIVE OIL OR BUTTER
2 TABLESPOONS ONION, MINCED
SALT AND PEPPER TO TASTE
5–6 CHERRY TOMATOES, SLICED IN HALF
½ CUP LEFTOVER PASTA
4 LARGE EGGS, BEATEN
2 TABLESPOONS PARMESAN CHEESE

OPTIONALS:
SMALL HANDFUL SHREDDED BASIL, IF YOU HAVE IT
   ON HAND (OR EVEN A SPRINKLE FROM A SPICE
   JAR)
RED PEPPER FLAKES, TO TASTE (TOTALLY OPTIONAL)

PREPARATION

1. Heat oil or butter in a skillet over a medium flame, add onions (and just a pinch of salt), and sauté for a couple of minutes, then follow with tomatoes (and another pinch of salt) and sauté for a few minutes longer.

2. Toss in pasta and stir together until pasta is warm, another minute or so.

3. Add beaten eggs, cheese, and basil and red pepper flakes, if using.

4. Scramble it all together until ready, or if you prefer, and you have the proficiency, allow it to set enough so that you can flip it over and present it as a sort of pancake-like omelet. Either way, serve it hot to happy campers. And don't tell them where the idea came from.

Killer Fruit Smoothies: 10 Things to Know

At some point, my kids starting requesting a smoothie every day at breakfast. From their perspective, it was about being sweet and delicious. From mine, it was an ideal way to get a whole lot of fruit into their bellies. The trick is to be able to do that without adding a bunch of unnecessary sugar. All you need is a blender. There are literally millions of possible combinations and permutations, so allow your own preferences to guide your experimentation.

Here are some suggestions from my experience.

1. You're going to need some kind of liquid to blend everything together harmoniously. (Unless you have one of those super-duper blenders that can make ANYTHING, including marbles, smooth.) Or UNLESS you use a fruit that liquefies immediately. Case in point: watermelon, which I've been using a lot these days for that very reason. The advantage of using watermelon is that it exudes so much liquid that I don't have to add any juice at all—which almost always contains sugar—before I blend in, say, a handful of frozen fruit. (One to two cups of watermelon provide plenty of juice, by the way.)

2. Your liquid of choice can be any juice, some form of milk (regular, almond, coconut, soy, etc.), or even water can be used. About 4 ounces per smoothie will usually suffice.

3. Fresh fruit or frozen works equally well. One advantage of the frozen option is that the fruit is ready to go, so you don't need to rinse, peel, and cut it. Just plop it right into the blender. I like to use frozen berries, peaches, pineapple, and especially a handful of cherries. (With berries, at some point you'll notice seeds stuck in your teeth. You could strain—I don't—or floss instead.)

4. Can you add veggies? Of course. Avocado works, and adds a creamy thickness; most greens work, too, but they can be a little bitter, which needs to be balanced by the sweetness of the fruit. So if you include kale, for example, try compensating with frozen cherries.

5. What about yogurt? For sure. Not only for health and creaminess, but also to offset the natural sweetness from the fruit.

6. How about peanut butter? You know it. Or almond butter. Not so much with fruit juice, but ideal when using the milks.

7. Speaking of sweetness and peanut butter, when we feel like something other than fruit only I make a smoothie with (unsweetened) almond milk, peanut butter, cocoa powder, and banana. It's awesome, but I find that it still needs a hit of sweetness, so I add a spoonful of agave syrup. Honey would be fine as well. But try it as is first because it might be sweet enough for your taste.

8. Ice is fine to add, too, especially when you're not using frozen fruit. No one wants a hot smoothie.

9. Pro tip: When you do go "all fruit," a squeeze of lemon or lime juice actually works to accentuate the fruit's sweetness.

10. Turns out there were only nine things. (Unless you count the idea that most every fruit-based smoothie is also conveniently converted into an adult beverage with the inclusion of vodka, rum, or tequila. This is strictly FYI; I'm certainly not advocating it for breakfast anyway. If interested, however, know that you might have to adjust the citrus/sweet balance with either fresh lemon or lime juice and your preferred sweetening agent.)

FRITTATA (INTUITIVE)

Frittata is the funky and fanciful name for an omelet-like dish filled with savory tidbits and baked so that it becomes like a quiche without a crust. Aside from its deliciousness, the best part for me is the number of variations possible, allowing you to use leftovers and/or other remnants you might find in the fridge. That includes virtually any kind of vegetable, potato, meats, cheeses, and herbs. As such, this is an "intuitive" dish in which eggs become the palette for your imagination. You can use leeks, mushrooms, asparagus, prosciutto, rice, goat cheese, salmon, potato, jarred red peppers . . . almost anything you have goes. (You can even use leftover pasta for your *frittata di pasta*!) The only caveat is not to overload it with too many goodies—five at the most—and, as always, don't overcook it, either. You want it to be a little fluffy rather than dried out. By the way, it's good for any mealtime, either hot or at room temp.

Notes:

1. Use an oven-safe pan that you can transfer from the top of the stove into oven. And remember that the larger the pan, the thinner the frittata, and the more quickly it will cook.

2. My basic recipe follows, but I repeat: make it yours. The thing to know is that I like using all already cooked ingredients because it's quicker and easier. However, if you choose to use raw ingredients (like bacon or sausage) you must cook them first and then remove from the pan to add back in later.

3. About the cheese: you can opt for different types of cheese depending on the texture you prefer. Cheddar and jack melt well; goat, feta, or ricotta make a creamy frittata; Parmesan offers a lot of taste, but neither meltability nor creaminess. You can surely use more than one type, and you can even put some on top of the frittata and finish it under the broiler for a minute or so to get a cheesy, crispy top.

SERVES 4

INGREDIENTS
6 LARGE EGGS
¼ CUP MILK (OPTIONAL, BUT PRODUCES
   A FLUFFIER FINAL RESULT)
½ CUP OR MORE SHREDDED CHEESE,
   PLUS MORE FOR "TOPPING"
1 TABLESPOON BUTTER OR OIL
⅓ CUP DICED ONION
⅓ CUP DICED RED OR GREEN BELL PEPPER
¾ CUP DICED COOKED POTATO
ABOUT ⅓ CUP CHOPPED COOKED BACON OR
   SAUSAGE
OPTIONAL: ½ TEASPOON HERB OR SPICE OF YOUR
   CHOICE (E.G. OREGANO, CHILI POWDER, ETC.)
½ TEASPOON SALT, OR TO TASTE, AND PEPPER

PREPARATION

1. Pre-heat the oven to 400°F.

2. Lightly beat together eggs with the milk (if using) and salt and pepper. Stir in the grated cheese and set aside.

3. In a 10–12 inch ovenproof skillet, melt butter or oil over medium-high heat. Add the onions and peppers and cook for several minutes, stirring frequently, until soft and beginning to brown. Spoon in diced potato and bacon, sprinkle with salt and pepper, stirring all together for a couple of minutes until everything is hot.

4. Evenly distribute ingredients across bottom of the pan and pour in the egg mixture, distributing it to coat everything. Cook on the burner for about a minute or until you see the edges begin to set, i.e., look like they're beginning to get a little firm. Then insert the skillet into the oven and keep an eye on it, watching for it to get somewhat firm, *but don't let it get too brown.* That might take about 8–12 minutes or so, depending on size and thickness. When it seems to be almost fully cooked, you can sprinkle cheese on top and place it under the broiler for just a minute.

5. Carefully remove the frittata from the skillet with the help of a spatula, onto a cutting board . . . or cut wedges out of the pan. But whatever you do, don't scratch that pan!

As mentioned, this stuff is good nice and hot, and perfectly fine at room temperature, too, even days later if you keep it in the refrigerator.

MORNING-AFTER POTATOES (A.K.A. HASH BROWNS)

Soft, yet crispy . . . salty and savory . . . who wouldn't want a side order of hash browns? Normally made on a flat top grill by the short order cook, hash browns define the diner breakfast experience. Here's the deal: I don't feel like making them from scratch. Especially at seven in the morning. Instead, bake up an extra potato or two at dinner and stick 'em in the fridge. Now all you need is a little bit of onion and green pepper chopped up (you could do that the night before too) and you're good to go.

Note: You know all that fat that renders (melts) out when you cook bacon? Well, you could save a bit of that to cook your hash browns in. Just saying . . .

INGREDIENTS
1½ TABLESPOONS OIL (OR BACON FAT; BUTTER WOULDN'T HURT EITHER)
½ SMALL ONION, CUT INTO DICE
½ GREEN PEPPER, CUT INTO DICE
2 MEDIUM BAKED POTATOES, CUT INTO BITE-SIZE PIECES
SALT AND PEPPER

PREPARATION

1. Heat up your pan and your fat of choice on medium high.

2. Sauté onion and pepper with a touch of salt and pepper until softened and fragrant, about 2–3 minutes.

3. Drop in the potatoes, spread 'em around, and toss 'em a little bit. You know, like you're having fun. When they get all brown and crispy, check your salt, and you're good to go.

OATMEAL BRÛLÉE

I've borrowed that crackling topping from the famous French dessert crème brûlée and applied to good old oatmeal. That sweet and crunchy effect has made it one of the current Short Order Dad favorites in our house. It happens to be high in fiber and protein, and it's filling, but best of all, it's also quite dramatic.

INGREDIENTS
1 PORTION OATMEAL
2 TEASPOONS SUGAR

Optional: nuts and/or raisins, to taste

PREPARATION

1. After cooking your oatmeal, stir in whatever other optional goodies (e.g., nuts or raisins) you like.

2. Pour it into a ramekin—which you can do ahead—and top it with a layer of sugar (about ⅛-inch thick).

3. Finish it under the broiler until it's brown and bubbling vigorously (3–4 minutes) for a sweet, crunchy effect kids dig, and dig into, big-time. It's high in fiber and protein, and it's filling, too. Best of all, it's highly dramatic.

Note: If you happen to have a blowtorch in your home, you can certainly use that! (Or splurge on one of those handy little kitchen torches.)

PINEAPPLE UPSIDE-DOWN PANCAKES

More of weekend thing, but this is a big hit. The nice part is that you can either use fresh pineapple and your own pancake mix made from scratch OR use pineapple slices right out of the can and pancake mix from a box. (Like I did. Just as good.) Either way, take my word on this: it's really hard not to like pineapple slices that have been caramelized/candied and incorporated into pancakes. You can make these individually or, if you're serving a few folks, I'd suggest making one big pancake in a pan that can go in the oven . . . and have enough to serve four people. Don't fret if you make more than you need; it's fine the next day, even cold.

INGREDIENTS

1½ TABLESPOONS BUTTER

4 SLICES OF PINEAPPLE CUT INTO ROUNDS (CORE REMOVED)

1½ TABLESPOONS SUGAR

PANCAKE BATTER FOR 4 PANCAKES

PREPARATION

1. Melt butter in a big ol' pan that you can put in the oven, like cast-iron. Lay down the pineapple in a single layer. Sprinkle with sugar. Let cook over medium heat for a couple of minutes, until you smell greatness. Pour favorite pancake batter over the top. Place in 375°F oven for 10–12 minutes until it's puffy, browned, and caramelized underneath.

2. Remove carefully and top it with real maple syrup, maybe a hit of powdered sugar. Feed people. Notice joy.

PEANUT BUTTER FRENCH TOAST

It Ain't Stuffed, Either

Truth be told, I don't make this often, but when I do I'm always blown away by how good it is. Then again, what could possibly be bad about combining creamy peanut butter with the sweet, fluffy goodness of French toast? Nothing. There's more than one way to do it, and as you know by now, I'm opting for the less complicated. That means that instead of stuffing two slices of bread with peanut butter, you blend the peanut butter directly into the egg mixture, drop in a couple of other flavor accents, and then soak your bread and cook it up as you always would. This stuff rocks!

INGREDIENTS

½ CUP MILK

2 EGGS

¼ CUP PEANUT BUTTER

½ TEASPOON VANILLA EXTRACT

¼ TEASPOON GROUND CINNAMON

1 TABLESPOON BUTTER

2 PIECES BREAD

PREPARATION

1. Whisk together milk, eggs, peanut butter, vanilla, and cinnamon in a large bowl until well blended.

2. Melt the butter in a frying pan or on a griddle over medium high heat. Soak each slice of bread in liquid mixture, both sides.

3. Cook on both sides until sizzling brown, about 2–3 minutes per side.

4. Serve with maple syrup or powdered sugar. Or have it with jam or jelly instead. Ever try that Stonewall Kitchen Pink Grapefruit Marmalade? Wow.

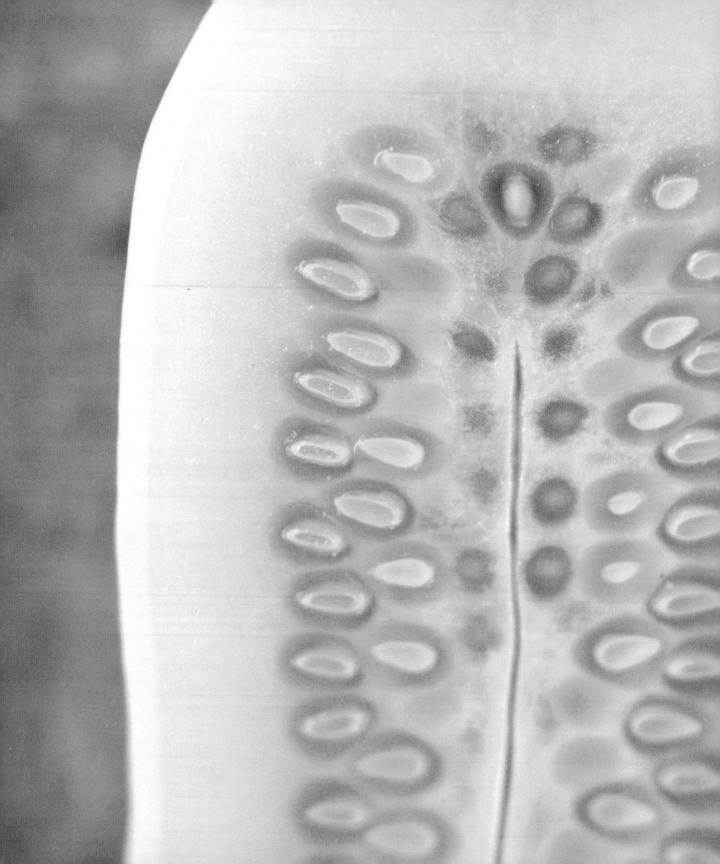

CHAPTER SEVEN

APPS AND SNACKS (GOOD FOR THE KIDS OR GREAT FOR THE DATE)

GO-TO GUACAMOLE

You MUST make your own guacamole. It will be 100 times better and fresher than what you can find already prepared in a grocery store. And you get to decide precisely how you like it. Smooth or chunky. Spicy or not. With or without other added ingredients, like tomatoes, for example.

Some things to know:

1. I am not a proponent of tomato in guacamole, a commonly added ingredient. For one thing, the star of this dish is obviously the avocado, and to me anyway, tomato detracts from that. For another, one of the great Mexican chefs I know (Betty Vasquez) told me, "Never add tomatoes." That's good enough for me.

2. As for the onion, you can use it as is, or you can give your chopped onion a quick rinse under cold water—then dry well—if you'd like to take some of the "bite" out of it.

3. My personal preference is a serrano chile pepper to a jalapeño because it's a little bit hotter and fruitier, but jalapeño is perfectly fine. And don't worry about the seeds so much; most of the spicy heat actually comes from the white pith (or "ribs") of the pepper. (By the way, in case you don't know: when you cut hot pepper, *keep your hands away from your eyes*. Wash hands well, wear gloves, do whatever it takes . . . but realize that if you accidentally rub your eyes while you have pepper on your fingers, plan on crying for the next hour.)

4. Don't overdo the lime juice. People have a tendency to go too heavy with it. Start with a little, taste, and you can always add more. Same with salt.

5. Of course you can buy tortilla chips, BUT, here's an option to consider: buy a package of corn tortillas instead, and put them in the oven—let's say 375°F—until they're crispy. There, you've made your own!

Now go get some *ripe* avocados and make guacamole today!!

YIELD: 3 CUPS

INGREDIENTS

3 RIPE HASS AVOCADOS
3 TABLESPOONS FINELY DICED RED ONION
1 LIME, JUICED (APPROXIMATELY 2 TABLESPOONS FRESHLY SQUEEZED JUICE), OR TO TASTE
1 FRESH SERRANO OR JALAPEÑO CHILE, SEEDED AND FINELY MINCED
1 CLOVE GARLIC, FINELY MINCED (OPTIONAL)
1 TEASPOON KOSHER SALT, OR TO TASTE
2–3 TABLESPOONS FRESH CILANTRO, CHOPPED OR TORN BY HAND

PREPARATION

1. Cut the avocados in half, the long way, remove the pits, and scoop the flesh into a large mixing bowl.

2. Add the remaining ingredients and mash using either or fork, a potato masher, or whatever other device you choose to reach the texture you find ideal. A little chunkiness is good. Taste, adjust the seasoning as needed, and serve immediately.

NUTS OF GLORY
(ROASTED, SPICED, AND GLAZED)

I love a good nut. Especially one that's salty and spicy with a hint of sweetness. I will actually choose one cocktail bar over another if they offer superior nuts. Who doesn't want superior nuts?

The concept is simple: Roasting makes a marked improvement to basic raw nuts. You can even do this in a toaster oven. The spice mixture can be blended to your taste specifications. For example, I like chili powder, cinnamon, and smoked paprika . . . but you can just as easily use cumin, curry, cayenne, or whatever else floats your boat. Just don't burn the nuts, which I seem to do about 50 percent of the time.

Pro Tip: Remember that not only does sweet stuff burn easily, it also sticks to the bottom of the pan. So if you want an easier cleanup, lay down a sheet of parchment paper in the roasting tray.

MAKES: ENOUGH FOR A SMALL CROWD

INGREDIENTS
2 CUPS (ABOUT 1 POUND) UNSALTED SHELLED NUTS (CAN MIX ALMONDS, CASHEWS, PECANS, WALNUTS, ETC.)

1 TABLESPOON OIL (NOT OLIVE, BUT A NEUTRAL OR PEANUT OIL) OR MELTED BUTTER

1½–2 TABLESPOONS HONEY (CAN SUBSTITUTE WITH DARK BROWN SUGAR OR MAPLE SYRUP)

½ TEASPOON SALT

1 TEASPOON SPICE MIX (TRY CINNAMON, SMOKED PAPRIKA, ANCHO CHILE POWDER, AND CAYENNE, TO TASTE)

PREPARATION

1. Pre-heat oven to 400°F.

2. Moisten the nuts with the oil (or butter) and honey, then toss in salt and spice mix to coat.

3. Scatter across a baking sheet and roast until lightly browned, about 10 minutes or so.

4. Remove them while hot. They'll get crisp and crackling as they cool, so let them do that before diving in.

YES YOU CAN-NELLINI (CREAMY WHITE BEAN DIP)

Really easy and remarkably flavorsome, this dip only requires a few ingredients and a blender. You can certainly adapt it to your own taste by including favorite herbs and spices. It's good straight on crackers or veggies, but would also work well smeared inside a wrap or on a sandwich with some roasted vegetables as well. It can also be made a day ahead and kept covered in the fridge.

MAKES ABOUT 1¼ CUPS

INGREDIENTS

1 15-OUNCE CAN CANNELLINI BEANS, DRAINED AND RINSED
1½ TABLESPOONS FRESH LEMON JUICE
1½ (OR MORE) TABLESPOONS EXTRA-VIRGIN OLIVE OIL
1 LARGE GARLIC CLOVE, PEELED
SALT AND PEPPER TO TASTE

PREPARATION

Puree first 4 ingredients in blender or processor until almost smooth. Season with salt and pepper. Maybe more lemon.

FRY ME A LIVER (SIMPLY SAUTÉED CHICKEN LIVERS)

Let's face it, chicken livers have an image problem. They're one of those polarizing foods that people either love or hate. I'm a lover. (If you know what I mean.) I firmly believe that more people would be enjoying them if they were served a little bit pink on the inside rather than being cooked to the point where they taste like, well . . . liver. When overcooked, liver becomes metallic and *minerally tasting.* Again, the key is to know when to pull it from the pan. Although that will depend, as always, on the size of the livers and the heat beneath them, my suggestion is to cook plump ones for maybe 3–4 minutes on medium high heat and then take one out and check for readiness. You're looking for a well-browned exterior, with just a touch of pink peeking through from the inside. Great as a shared appetizer or good for a small meal with couple of eggs or a few tomatoes and slice of baguette.

SERVES 2 OR 4 AS AN APPETIZER

INGREDIENTS
1 POUND OF CHICKEN LIVERS
SALT AND PEPPER TO TASTE
2 TABLESPOONS OLIVE OIL OR BUTTER

PREPARATION

1. Lightly rinse livers, remove any fat or membranes you see, and slice them into separate "lobes." Pat dry well with paper towels. Sprinkle with salt and grind pepper all around the livers.

2. Heat the olive oil or butter (until it's melted and foaming) in the skillet over medium-high heat, and place the livers in one layer without crowding them. Cook for 2 minutes on one side until they're browned, then turn them over and cook another minute or 2 on the other side until browned. Check for doneness. They should be slightly pink inside.

TOASTY BRUSCHETTA

Bruschetta is basically the fancy Italian way to say *toast*. But it may be the best toast you've ever had. Actually, the word itself means *a little charred*, and that's what you're looking for when you cook it, the slightest char. Then you can top it off with any one of a number of options, from the simplest—rubbed with garlic, painted with olive oil, a touch of coarse salt—to everything from tomatoes, beans (like that white bean dip on page 83), cheese, vegetables, prosciutto, or whatever your imagination allows. It's a great appetizer, especially for parties, and can be prepared in very little time.

FYI: The proper Italian pronunciation is *broo–skett–ah*.

INGREDIENTS

RUSTIC ITALIAN BREAD OR A FRENCH BAGUETTE,
   CUT INTO SLICES ABOUT ½-INCH THICK
2 GARLIC CLOVES, PEELED AND CUT IN HALF
   LENGTHWISE
¼ CUP EXTRA-VIRGIN OLIVE OIL
SALT TO TASTE

PREPARATION

1. Preheat oven to 400°F.

2. Place bread on baking sheet and toast until, well, a little charred. A little.

3. Rub the toasts with the peeled garlic clove. It's like you're buttering, but you're actually "garlicking."

4. Drizzle oil over bruschetta and garnish with either nothing but a pinch of salt or whatever your heart desires, as mentioned above.

Yield: As many ½-inch toasts as your loaf of bread allows.

DIY (THIN CRUST) PIZZA (INTUITIVE)

You've got to try this. Everyone loves pizza and there's something exciting about making and customizing your own. This one's especially quick, easy, and rewarding. The surprise element is the use of a flour tortilla as the "dough." Why? It uses essentially the same predominant ingredients as a regular pizza dough—flour and water—and produces a crackling thin crust. All you really need is some sauce and cheese . . . plus a skillet you can stick under the broiler in the oven for a minute to two. Have fun choosing whatever (quick-cooking) toppings you love.

SERVES 1 TO 2

INGREDIENTS
EXTRA-VIRGIN OLIVE OIL

LARGE FLOUR TORTILLA (THAT FITS IN YOUR PAN)

2–3 TABLESPOONS TOMATO SAUCE (SEE MINE ON PAGE 149, OR STORE-BOUGHT)

2 OUNCES SHREDDED MOZZARELLA CHEESE

1–2 OUNCES GRATED PARMESAN CHEESE

2 BASIL LEAVES, ROUGHLY TORN

Optional toppings: red onion, sliced bell peppers, pepperoni, prosciutto, red pepper flakes, etc.

PREPARATION

1. Adjust top rack in oven about 8 inches from broiler and turn the broiler on. Place a large cast-iron skillet over medium-high heat.

2. Very lightly brush both sides of one tortilla with olive oil. Place tortilla in skillet and spread sauce all over it. Evenly spread mozzarella and half of Parmesan on tortilla. Drizzle with a touch of olive oil and top with a basil leaves.

3. Using a spatula, check to see that underside of tortilla is starting to brown. Then place skillet under broiler until cheese is melted and beginning to brown, about 2 minutes.

4. Remove from oven onto cutting board. Sprinkle on remaining Parmesan, if desired. Slice and serve immediately.

Pizza

If you don't happen to be into super-thin crust pizza, allow me to suggest this alternative: pick up a premade pizza dough, frozen or not. Even better, buy one directly from your neighborhood pizza maker. Seriously, if your pizza shop will sell you dough, go for it. If that's the case, the ingredients above are still valid, but the proportion and process will fundamentally change.

If you buy a pizza dough you'll need to spread it out. You can cook in a baking pan/sheet, or directly on a pizza stone or one of those perforated nonstick pizza pans. If it's the baking pan, lightly lubricate it first with oil. Then, using some combination of a rolling pin and your own hands, spread the dough as far as possible to the edges of the pan. If you have good dough, it is often quite elastic, which can make it challenging to spread. *Get the dough to room temperature first*, and be patient, but try not to handle the dough too much because a) you will tear it and b) it will get tough rather than chewy. And you want chewy. So the more you can stretch the dough before you lay it in the pan, the better. I'd pre-bake that dough for a few minutes until it starts to firm up. Only a few minutes, and you'll smell it. Then add the sauce and toppings and cook on very high heat until crust is browned, cheese is melted, and toppings are cooked!

MANNY, MO, AND JACK (QUESADILLAS WITH PROSCIUTTO, MONTEREY JACK, AND MANCHEGO)

That's **man**go salsa with a **mo**jito and a **jack** cheese quesadilla. A righteous combination of big flavors, easy to assemble, and all washed down with one of the best things to come out of Cuba since Gloria Estefan. Nothing wrong with that. For Mojito, see recipe on page 244.

SERVES 4

INGREDIENTS
FOUR 6- TO 7-INCH FLOUR TORTILLAS
¼ POUND THINLY SLICED PROSCIUTTO
½ CUP COARSELY GRATED MONTEREY JACK
½ CUP COARSELY GRATED MANCHEGO

PREPARATION

1. Place tortilla in nonstick fry pan.

2. Top with half of the prosciutto and half of both cheeses.

3. Press another tortilla on top and place over medium high heat until golden brown on one side, 2–3 minutes.

4. Flip onto the other side until browned and cheese has melted.

5. Repeat the whole process again with the balance of the ingredients.

6. Slice in wedges and serve with mango salsa and a cold beer or cocktail.

MANGO SALSA
(for Mango Tomato Salsa, see recipe on page 202)

SERVES 6

INGREDIENTS
2 RIPE MANGOES, PEELED AND CHOPPED INTO BITE-SIZE PIECES
1 JALAPEÑO, SEEDED AND FINELY CHOPPED
2 TABLESPOONS RED ONION, FINELY CHOPPED
LARGE HANDFUL OF CILANTRO, CHOPPED
1–2 LIMES, FOR JUICING
SALT

PREPARATION
Mix all ingredients in a bowl and let sit for 30 minutes or more.

PIGS IN BLANKETS

Have you ever noticed that no matter what other types of hors d'oeuvres are served at fancy catered affairs—whether it's shrimp cocktail, caviar, or sliced steak—guests will run over a bride to get to the pigs in blankets? I've been making this classic for a while and it's always a hit with the crowd. Plus, it's *only two ingredients*, both of which are bought at your local supermarket. Although pigs in blankets are meant to be small, I bake these huge, encasing an entire kielbasa in all the dough it takes to envelop it, before cutting it into bite-size pieces for serving. What more do you need to know? That rather than calling them pigs in blankets, you might refer to them by their fancy French name, *saucisson en croûte.* People seem to like that even more.

APPETIZER FOR 4 OR MORE

INGREDIENTS

1 LARGE POLISH KIELBASA (SUCH AS HILLSHIRE FARM)

1 (8 OZ.) CAN PILLSBURY REFRIGERATED CRESCENT DINNER ROLLS

Note: If you can find it, buy the Crescent Recipe Creations Seamless Dough Sheet. That said, I've never once actually seen it in stores. So get the Grands! Crescent Big & Flaky, which is 50 percent larger.

PREPARATION

1. Preheat oven to temperature indicated on package. Sear the kielbasa in a medium hot skillet until it's well browned, then remove and let it cool.

2. Cut the dough in half lengthwise, and using a rolling pin and all the skill you've got, roll out the dough wide enough to encase the entire kielbasa. Fold the dough around the kielbasa so that it's entirely enclosed. If that takes two separate pieces of dough, fine. If that's the case, just pinch the pieces together. To minimize big, ugly seams of dough, if you see them, place them facedown on a baking sheet.

3. Bake following package directions. (Usually 375°F for 12 to 15 minutes.) When beautifully browned, remove from oven and slice into bite-size pieces. Serve with your favorite mustard. Tell the bride to move out of the way.

CRUNCHY COLD CUCUMBER CHUNKS

Is this even a recipe? I vacillated over whether or not to include because it seems so obvious and simple that I feel a little guilty. Yet . . . when we went to an Italian restaurant not too long ago, this is exactly what they brought to the table instead of the usual bread and butter. And you know what? It was so good. Especially for me, because I don't even love cucumbers and don't include them in my salads. But when you have a good firm one, and you remove the seeds (easily accomplished with a spoon), then cut it into nice, large chunks, douse it with a good splash of quality olive oil, and sprinkle it with sea salt . . . you have a revelation. One that's crunchy, tasty, and healthy. They're best good and cold.

INGREDIENTS
1–2 LARGE CUCUMBERS, PEELED AND SEEDED*
2–3 GOOD "GLUGS" OF BEST QUALITY OLIVE OIL
CRUNCHY SALT, SUCH AS MALDON SEA SALT OR
    KOSHER

PREPARATION

1. Cut cold cucumbers into large bite-size chunks.
2. Cover with oil and salt.
3. Serve cold.

*Those long "English" or "hothouse" cucumbers are particularly good for this because their seeds are so small they don't have to be removed. Regular cukes are just as good, but I think better when the seeds are removed. So peel them, cut them in half lengthwise, and simply scrape out the seeds using a spoon.

CHAPTER EIGHT

RED MEAT, PIG, AND POULTRY (IT'S ALL GOOD IN SMALL DOSES)

ROAST LEG OF LAMB

Three ingredients to greatness. (Four if you count pepper. But come on, who's counting pepper?) You could buy lamb on the bone, which is ordinarily the better way to go because bones bring flavor. But I'm going the lazy route here by using boneless because I think it's even less work. In fact, I don't even bother unrolling the lamb and removing anything that looks inedible—fat, sinew, or gristle—which you might do if you're not too lazy. And if you feel like doing another few minutes' work, and you have some fresh garlic and rosemary on hand, stuff 'em in there, too.

Note: This is one of those dishes that's perfectly scrumptious on its own (see page 96), yet you can always bring a little something extra to the table. Literally. *Gremolata* (page 208) is an assertive mixture of parsley, lemon zest, and garlic, and if you favor big flavor, a little bit of it on top of a nice piece of lamb could be mighty fine.

6–8 SERVINGS

INGREDIENTS
¼ CUP SOY SAUCE

¼ CUP DIJON MUSTARD

5-POUND BONELESS LEG OF LAMB

1 TEASPOON FRESHLY GROUND BLACK PEPPER, OR
   TO TASTE

3 CLOVES GARLIC, SLICED (OPTIONAL, BUT GOOD)

1 TABLESPOON CHOPPED FRESH ROSEMARY
   (OPTIONAL)

PREPARATION

1. Preheat oven to 400°F.

2. Blend soy sauce and Dijon mustard together. Rub the entire lamb with the marinade. Crack black pepper over. (If using garlic and/or rosemary fold it into the lamb so that it's not exposed directly to the heat.) Roast lamb in a shallow baking dish until internal temp at the thickest part reaches at least 130–135°F for medium rare, 140–145°F for medium.

3. Cover with foil and rest. You AND the lamb; you've worked hard. Fifteen minutes later, slice and serve. Perhaps with some nice potatoes and a side of greens. Maybe some *gremolata* (page 208). Plus a glass of Côtes du Rhône for the grown-ups.

WORLD'S BEST BEER-BRAISED BRISKET OF BEEF

This delicious and simple recipe transforms an ordinary piece of meat into an extraordinary meal. And there are 10 good reasons to do it.

1. It is easy to make. (And hard to screw up.)
2. It's inexpensive.
3. It requires only one pot.
4. It produces its own glorious gravy.
5. It makes your house smell really, really good.
6. It's at least as good the next day. ("It makes a nice sandwich.")
7. It can feed a lot of people.
8. It's an extremely adaptable recipe.
9. Everyone loves it—kids and grown-ups alike. (Vegetarians, not so much.)
10. Most important, it's mouthwateringly delicious and fall-off-the-bone tender. And there's not even a bone.

Yes, my friends: say hello to Beer-Braised Brisket of Beef. The name *brisket* itself may not be sexy, but the dish is. You need only a few things to proceed:

- Large pot with a tight-fitting lid that's big enough to house the hunk of meat you're about to cook. It is generally called a stockpot or the more interesting sounding Dutch oven.
- The meat, onions, garlic, some type of tomato product, and beer. Salt, pepper, and oil also come into play.
- A little bit of patience; magnificence can't be rushed.

Here's the process, broken down:

The amount of brisket obviously depends on how many eaters; figure about ¾ pound uncooked per person, but I'd encourage more because leftovers rock. The onion and garlic add a lot of flavor, so I use plenty of both, particularly the onions, which benefit from long cooking to become sweet and soft. By "tomato product" I mean some form of canned tomato. It can be whole tomatoes, crushed, pureed, or tomato paste, any of which will add color and taste to the mix. Don't tell anyone, but I've also used ketchup successfully.

The beer is used to "braise" the meat, which means slow cooking in liquid. With sufficient heat and time, the alcohol will cook out of the beer but leave behind a rich flavor. So you might want to splurge on something fuller bodied, like an amber beer. But if you prefer to make this without beer, you can easily substitute beef or vegetable broth and still achieve delicious results. (Red wine works, too.)

The bit about patience. Once you handle the simple pregame prep, which involves some slicing, seasoning, and searing, your brisket becomes like a reluctant starlet who wants to be left alone—at least for a couple of hours. But that's good, too. Life is fast enough; dinner shouldn't have to be.

Now for the game plan:

SERVES 6

1. GET YOUR INGREDIENTS
1 BEEF BRISKET (ABOUT 3 POUNDS)
2 GARLIC CLOVES, PEELED AND SLICED THIN
1 TABLESPOON SALT AND GROUND BLACK PEPPER TO TASTE
2 TABLESPOONS VEGETABLE OIL
2–3 BOTTLES LAGER OR AMBER BEER (CAN SUBSTITUTE WITH 3–4 CUPS BEEF OR VEGETABLE BROTH)
4 LARGE ONIONS, PEELED AND SLICED
10-OUNCE CAN CRUSHED TOMATOES OR 1 SMALL CAN OF TOMATO PASTE
½ TEASPOON CAYENNE PEPPER OR HOT HUNGARIAN PAPRIKA (OPTIONAL, BUT NICE IF YOU LIKE A LITTLE KICK)

2. MAKE THE BRISKET
- Pat the brisket dry. With the tip of a sharp knife, make slits in both sides of the meat and stuff with thin slices of garlic. The more you like garlic, the more slits you'll make. Season each side very generously with ⅔ of the salt and pepper.
- Heat oil in a large, heavy bottomed pot over medium high flame. When hot, brown the brisket on both sides, lowering heat as necessary so as not to burn. You're looking for a nice brown color, not burnt. (And remember, don't burn the *sucs* collecting in the bottom of the pot.)
- When browned, add beer, onions, remaining salt, tomato product, and cayenne if you're using. There should be enough liquid to cover about ⅔ of the brisket. If you need more liquid, you can also use broth to supplement the beer. Stir and bring mixture to boil, then lower the flame so that broth remains "simmering," i.e., not vigorous, but still moving gently. Cover the pot. (You can leave it on top of stove OR place in a 350°F preheated oven.)
- Cook until meat is very tender but not totally falling apart, at least two hours. More is fine. Just make sure to check along the way to ensure that you still have sufficient liquid in the pot to partially cover the meat. Add more if necessary.

- Remove brisket to a carving board and cover it with aluminum foil. Now look at the remaining oniony broth/gravy and decide if you like what you see or you would like it to be thicker. If there is a lot of liquid, you can reduce it considerably by putting it back on the stove top, at a higher temperature, and reduce with heat until it reaches the consistency you desire. That could take a good 20 minutes IF you have a lot of liquid in the pot. Taste and adjust seasoning, adding more salt or pepper if necessary. Then slice brisket AGAINST the grain and top with onion gravy.

3. ADD THE FINISHING TOUCHES

Serve alongside something that will welcome all the sauce, like mashed potatoes, noodles, couscous, or a baguette and some bagged salad greens with a sprinkle of olive oil, lemon, and salt.

Once you understand the basic technique of searing and braising you can customize your own version with a variety of flavorful additions that excite you—40 cloves of garlic, herbs like thyme or a little rosemary, spices such as cumin, cinnamon, or curry powder, red wine instead of beer, dried apricots, or carrots and parsnips added during the last hour of cooking.

If you're not in the mood for brisket, go ahead and braise short ribs. Or a shoulder of pork. The concept is the same: season and sear the meat, add aromatics like garlic and onion, and then cook slowly in a flavorful liquid until it gets as tender as you are tough. Now rejoice and eat meat!

OSSO BUCO

Okay, you've made it this far, so here's a recipe that's just a tad ambitious. Not too complicated for the likes of you, but it calls for the most ingredients of any recipe in the book. Why? Because when osso buco is good, it's great. And when you make it yourself, it's even better. It falls off the bone, the sauce is killer, and it's hugely impressive. The concept: dust the veal shanks with seasoned flour, brown them, add aromatic vegetables, and braise in wine and stock enhanced by tomato and herbs. Go ahead, you can do it.

SERVES 4

INGREDIENTS
1 CUP FLOUR
SALT AND PEPPER TO TASTE
4 VEAL SHANKS (ABOUT 2½ POUNDS)
1½ TABLESPOONS OLIVE OIL
½ CUP DRY WHITE WINE
1 MEDIUM ONION, DICED (ABOUT A CUP)
2 CARROTS, PEELED AND DICED (ABOUT A CUP)
1 CELERY STALK, DICED (¾ CUP)
4 MEDIUM GARLIC CLOVES, CHOPPED (4 TABLESPOONS)
½ TEASPOON DRIED OREGANO
2 SPRIGS THYME
2 BAY LEAVES
3 TABLESPOONS TOMATO PASTE
1 CUP CHICKEN STOCK (LOW SALT IS BEST)
CHOPPED PARSLEY, FOR GARNISH

PREPARATION

1. Preheat oven to 350°F.

2. Combine flour, salt, and pepper, dredge the shanks with the flour mixture, and shake off any excess.

3. Heat oil in large heavy ovenproof casserole or Dutch oven over medium-high heat. Brown the veal in batches, on both sides. Remove it to a plate and continue until all the veal is browned. Use more oil along the way if you need.

4. When veal is browned, drain any excess oil from pot.

5. Pour in wine and cook over medium heat, scraping up the browned bits from the bottom. (This is not a test, but if you've been following along, I believe you know what those are called by now.)

6. Stir in onion, carrots, celery, garlic, oregano, thyme, bay leaves, and tomato paste and give a swirl around.

7. Now return the veal to the pot and pour in the chicken stock (should come about 2/3 of the way up the veal).

8. Add salt and pepper.

9. Bring the mixture to a boil, then cover and cook it in the oven for about an hour until falling off the bone. Literally. That is, you can actually see the veal separating from the bone

10. . . . but do remove and serve it attached, in a bowl with sauce and veggies.

11. Garnish with parsley. Great with risotto (page 154) and *gremolata* on the side (page 208).

Red Meat, Pig, and Poultry (It's all good in small doses)

CHORIZO BEEF BURGER

Okay, to be honest, this is a few more ingredients than I would normally use or advise. BUT, I made it to enter it into some kind of contest and my own people enjoyed it a lot. Although it didn't win the contest, it turns out that the judges never actually tasted the burger, they were just evaluating it by the photo I had sent in. They missed out; you don't have to.

Note: The chorizo in this recipe is the raw kind. (More likely to be Mexican than Spanish.) It is soft, unlike the firm type that's already cooked or cured, similar to salami or pepperoni. And it often comes in links, in which case you would slice those open to remove the meat from its casing so that you can blend it with the hamburger meat. Therefore make sure you cook the burger well enough . . . and remember that you won't have to pre-salt the burger meat because there's already salt in the chorizo.

MAKES 4 HUGE BURGERS

INGREDIENTS
1 POUND GROUND SIRLOIN
1 POUND UNCOOKED CHORIZO SAUSAGE, GROUND
2 TABLESPOONS OLIVE OIL
2 MEDIUM ONIONS, SLICED
1 TEASPOON SPANISH PAPRIKA
1 TABLESPOON BROWN SUGAR
SALT AND PEPPER
2 TABLESPOONS MAYONNAISE
1 TABLESPOON SRIRACHA SAUCE
4 KAISER ROLLS
4 OUNCES GRATED MANCHEGO CHEESE

PREPARATION

1. In a large bowl, mix together the ground sirloin and raw chorizo meat. Set aside.

2. Heat two tablespoons of oil in a skillet over medium/medium-low heat. Sauté sliced onions, smoked paprika, and brown sugar with a touch of salt and pepper for about 10–15 minutes, until onions are golden brown. Set aside.

3. Mix together mayonnaise and sriracha. Set aside.

4. Preheat the grill for high heat. Form the meat into four patties. (The chorizo is already salty, so no need to add salt.)

5. Grill burgers for 5 minutes per side, or until done to your liking. Split buns in half and toast briefly on grill.

6. Smear a dollop of sriracha mayo on buns, then place burgers onto buns and top with caramelized onion and grated Manchego cheese.

7. Dig in!

MVP RIBS (CHINESE-SPICED BABY BACK RIBS)

If you enjoy the spare ribs at a Chinese restaurant you're going to like these as well. It's a simple two-step process I employ that yields finger-licking results. First you apply a dry rub and oven roast the ribs on low heat for a long time ("low and slow"). That gets them nice and soft. Then you brush them with a zesty marinade and finish them off on a grill or in the oven. In either case, these are a crowd-pleaser.

Note: This makes more than enough marinade for basting and for brushing on ribs when they're done. Since the ribs are cooked before applying the marinade there's no need to worry about using the same marinade for sauce.

SERVES 4–6, DEPENDING ON THE SIZE OF THE RACKS AND THE SIZE OF THE EATERS

INGREDIENTS

For the dry rub
2 TEASPOONS SALT
1 TEASPOON PEPPER
½ TEASPOON CHINESE FIVE-SPICE POWDER
2 RACKS BABY BACK PORK RIBS

For the marinade
½ CUP SOY SAUCE
1½ INCHES FRESH GINGER, PEELED
   AND COARSELY CHOPPED
2 CLOVES GARLIC, PEELED
2½ TABLESPOONS HONEY

PREPARATION

1. Preheat oven to 225°F.

2. Mix salt, pepper, and Chinese five-spice together.

3. Place ribs on a baking sheet and cover both sides well with dry rub.

4. Slow roast for approximately 2½–3 hours, turning them over once or twice along the way for even cooking.

5. Cook until brown and meat is tender enough to separate from the bone.

6. Blend together soy, ginger, garlic, and honey.

7. When ribs are ready, paint the marinade liberally on both sides.

8. At this point they can be finished over a hot grill or placed back in the oven under the broiler until well browned on both sides. Either way, apply additional marinade on the ribs when you turn them over.

9. Remove when sufficiently browned, brush with more marinade, and cut into individual ribs for serving. I'm thinking ice cold beer.

SEARED DUCK BREASTS OVER GREENS WITH WARM VINAIGRETTE

Totally underappreciated, thoroughly mouthwatering. We don't tend to think about duck that often as a dinner option. But if you can get your hands on some good quality duck breasts it is really worth it. Because it's more like red meat than chicken, do not overcook it. It's best medium rare. And you should save all the "rendered" fat that melts off during cooking because it's excellent for panfrying potatoes or using in a warm vinaigrette.

MAKES 4 SERVINGS

INGREDIENTS
4 BONELESS 8-OUNCE DUCK BREASTS (ANY WILL
    DO, BUT MUSCOVY IS VERY FLAVORFUL)
SALT AND PEPPER

For warm vinaigrette
1 TABLESPOON RESERVED DUCK FAT
2 TABLESPOONS OLIVE OIL
1 TABLESPOON SHERRY WINE VINEGAR (CAN
    SUBSTITUTE GOOD QUALITY RED WINE VINEGAR)
MIXED SALAD GREENS

PREPARATION

1. *Score* (cut) the fat on the breasts deeply in a crosshatch pattern *without piercing all the way through the skin to the breast meat underneath*. Season *aggressively* with salt and freshly cracked pepper.

2. In a medium hot pan (preferably heavy-bottomed, like cast-iron) sear breasts slowly, skin side down, to render out the fat, until the skin is crispy and caramel colored, about 10–12 minutes (more or less). Turn over and cook meat side another 2–3 minutes until medium rare (125°F). Set aside.

3. Reserve one tablespoon of duck fat in the sauté pan. Turn off heat and stir in olive oil and vinegar.

4. After a short rest, slice breasts and serve over mixed salad greens with warm vinaigrette.

BRAISED CHICKEN WITH 41 GARLIC CLOVES

Among the thousands of different ways to make chicken, what sets this one-pot dish above most others is the rich creaminess of the sauce that results from the happy marriage of wine, garlic, and the chicken itself. And while the 41 cloves of garlic might sound like a lot, they get soft, mellow, and sweet during cooking. Perhaps best of all, braising is a most forgiving cooking method with formidable results practically guaranteed.

MAKES 4 SERVINGS

INGREDIENTS
1 CHICKEN, CUT IN 8 PIECES
SALT AND PEPPER
2–3 TABLESPOONS OLIVE OIL
41 GARLIC CLOVES, SEPARATED BUT UNPEELED (OR GO CRAZY AND USE 42)
2 CUPS DRY WHITE WINE, SUCH AS PINOT GRIS
4 SPRIGS FRESH THYME, ROSEMARY, OR TARRAGON
HANDFUL OF CHOPPED PARSLEY, FOR GARNISH

PREPARATION

1. Season the chicken pieces well on all sides with salt and pepper.

2. In a large Dutch oven, warm half of the oil over medium high heat. Brown half the chicken pieces until the skin is golden, 6 to 7 minutes per side. Remove chicken and set aside; repeat step with the remaining oil and chicken.

3. Remove all but about 1 tablespoon of the remaining fat from the Dutch oven. Put in the garlic and sauté over medium heat until fragrant, about 1 minute.

4. Return the chicken, pour in the wine, and add the herbs.

5. Bring to a boil, then lower the heat and simmer, covered, until the chicken is cooked through and tender, about 35 minutes.

6. Transfer the chicken pieces to a platter, and reduce the cooking juices to about 1 cup, about 5–10 minutes.

7. Adjust the seasoning with salt and pepper to taste.

8. Pour the sauce over chicken, garnish with parsley, and serve immediately.

ROAST CHICKEN WITH A LOTTA LEMON AND GARLIC SAUCE

At some point you're going to want to make a great roast chicken. Although it's not complicated, to be totally blunt, it's not always as simple as it sounds to get it just right, either. That may be why so many chefs and food professionals judge cooks by their ability to make a perfect roast chicken. What makes it perfect? Flavor, of course, as well as meat that maintains its juiciness and skin that crackles when you bite into it.

Although all you really need is salt, pepper, and heat, lemon and garlic add a lot of flavor and a TON of jus. *Herbes de Provence* are a wonderful addition, but optional if you don't have. Instead, you could certainly insert a few sprigs of rosemary, thyme, or tarragon directly into the cavity and allow their perfume to penetrate the bird.

Notes:

1. I'm big on high heat roasting because I want super crispy skin. So don't be surprised if the fire alarm goes off. That just means that you have to keep your eye on the chicken as it's roasting. If you see the skin getting too dark, you can either lower the heat and cook slightly longer, or cover the chicken with a lid (or foil), which I prefer, because that preserves the accumulated juices.

2. *Herbes de Provence* is simply a blend of fragrant, dried herbs typically found in the southwest of France. Although readily available in supermarkets, you can easily make your own by mixing equal parts of any or all of these: rosemary, thyme, oregano, savory, and marjoram.

3. Get under the skin. What makes this chicken so flavorful comes from the lemon and garlic, some of which should be applied directly to the chicken meat underneath the skin. That requires that you loosen and lift the skin. Here's how: With the breast side facing up, and entering at the bottom part of the chicken, left the skin away from the meat. Working slowly and gently—you don't want to tear the skin—slide your fingers between the skin and the meat to separate as much and as far back as you can reach. In a way, you're creating a pocket between chicken and skin.

4. The choice of cooking vessel matters. There will be some be some tradeoff between the amount of jus (juice) that collects and the degree of crispy skin you can attain. I come out on the middle on this one. That is, I'm willing to sacrifice the crispy skin on the underside of the chicken (the thighs) in exchange for the quantity of jus. Therefore, I roast this breast-side-up only, in an enamel casserole-type dish that surrounds the chicken and allows juices to collect during cooking. An oval Dutch oven would be good as well (and I bet you could effectively use a glass Pyrex one, too). Although it could be argued that this is not true roasting, which is characterized by dry heat cooking exclusively, it's not the definition I'm concerned about here. It's the chicken. So . . . if you want a boatload of flavorful, lemony, garlicky juices in which to dip your chicken pieces, cook it in something that surrounds the chicken, thus allowing the liquid to accumulate. (A lot of which will eventually end up running down your chin.) If, on the other hand, you are more interested in attaining super crispy skin all over the bird, then roasting it on a flatter, open surface (or on a "roasting rack") should evaporate a lot of the juices during cooking and allow all the skin to be more exposed to the dry heat that renders it crispy. In that case, just remember that to achieve even roasting and crisping on both sides, you'll either need to turn the chicken over half-way through the roasting, or elevate the chicken on a roasting rack during cooking so that all the skin is exposed directly to the dry heat.

SERVES 4

INGREDIENTS

1 BROILER CHICKEN, ABOUT 3½ POUNDS

EXTRA-VIRGIN OLIVE OIL (OPTIONAL)

2 TEASPOONS KOSHER SALT

1 TEASPOON FRESHLY GROUND BLACK PEPPER

1½ TEASPOONS HERBES DE PROVENCE (OR OTHER DRIED HERBS SUCH AS ROSEMARY, THYME, OR TARRAGON)

4–5 CLOVES GARLIC, PEELED, CRUSHED AND CHOPPED

JUICE AND ZEST OF 2 LEMONS (AND RESERVE THE "USED" LEMONS)

PREPARATION

1. Heat the oven to 450°F. Rinse the chicken inside and out and make sure you dry it very well with paper towels.

2. If using, drizzle the chicken with a little stream of olive oil.

3. Mix the salt, pepper, and herbs together and spread most of it all over and inside the chicken. Place most of the garlic in the cavity. Take the rest of it, together with the rest of the seasoning, and insert under the skin, as described above.

4. Pour lemon juice and place lemon zest all over and around the chicken. Put the "used" lemon pieces into the cavity.

5. Roast for about 60 minutes or so, until the chicken is very crisp and the meat cooked through. (Remember the note above about covering if necessary.) The chicken is done when the juices from the thigh run clear. (To be safe, the government says that chicken is fully cooked at 165°F. That means to ensure juicy chicken, you should pull it out at 160 and let the "residual heat" finish the job.)

6. Let it rest for 15 minutes, then carve and serve proudly in the pan or on a platter. You might even want to serve the collected juices in their own gravy bowl.

BAKED CHICKEN PARMIGIANA

Chicken Parm is a lovable dish. The typical restaurant version can be kind of heavy, but my version is lighter and leaner because the chicken is baked rather than fried. Plus I avoid the usual time and mess of breading by sticking strictly to olive oil as the "glue" to adhere bread crumbs to the breasts.

Note: Cooking time will depend entirely on the thickness of your chicken breasts.

SERVES 4

INGREDIENTS
4 SKINLESS, BONELESS CHICKEN BREASTS
2 TABLESPOONS OF OLIVE OIL
SALT AND PEPPER TO TASTE
1 CUP OF BREAD CRUMBS
1 CUP TOMATO SAUCE (SEE PAGE 149)
4 OUNCES MOZZARELLA CHEESE, SHREDDED
   OR SLICED

PREPARATION
1. Preheat oven at 425°F.

2. Coat chicken breasts with olive oil and season with salt and pepper. Roll and press the chicken into crumbs, adhering bread crumbs to both sides of breasts to coat as well as possible.

3. Position breasts onto nonstick baking sheet and into oven. When crumbs begin to brown (about 10 minutes) carefully turn chicken over and continue baking until bread crumbs are browned and crisp and chicken is cooked through. Top the chicken pieces with tomato sauce and mozzarella cheese. Place under broiler and cook until cheese is bubbling.

HONEY, SOY, AND GINGER CRISPY LACQUERED CHICKEN

Like most Americans, we eat a lot of chicken. So there's a never-ending search to find new ways to make it. For me, that involves my usual formula: *the most taste, with the fewest ingredients and the least effort* ™. In this case, I dedicate five ingredients to what they might call a Chinese flavor profile (soy, ginger, garlic, sesame oil, and Chinese five-spice). These are blended with honey and painted on the bird in order to end up with skin so crisp you can hear it when it cracks.

What you need to know: The key again is Heat Management, riding that fine line between crisp and burnt. Because sweet stuff burns. When using sugar, or in this case, honey in the marinade, you must take extra care to avoid burning because sugars can burn before the underlying protein is ready. Although you could roast for a longer time on a lower heat, I find that the best way to ensure super crispy skin is to start with high heat. But you've got to be vigilant. So keep your eye on the prize as it roasts, baste it with marinade along the way, and turn down the heat when you see the skin becoming brown enough. You also have the option of covering the chicken—with a lid or aluminum foil—so that you can keep cooking without burning. You want to end up with a fully cooked chicken and a beautifully lacquered, mahogany-colored skin that cracks like thin glass.

SERVES 4

INGREDIENTS

For marinade
2–3 GARLIC CLOVES
1½-INCHES FRESH GINGER, PEELED AND COARSELY CHOPPED (APPROXIMATELY 2 TABLESPOONS)
¼ CUP TAMARI SAUCE* (CAN SUBSTITUTE DARK SOY SAUCE)
½ TEASPOON CHINESE FIVE-SPICE POWDER
¼ TEASPOON SESAME OIL
2 TABLESPOONS HONEY

3½-POUND CHICKEN, WHOLE, BUTTERFLIED, OR CUT INTO PIECES (BROUGHT TO ROOM TEMPERATURE BEFORE ROASTING)

PREPARATION

1. Preheat oven to 450°F.
2. In a blender, combine all marinade ingredients and buzz until well blended.
3. Brush all sides of chicken well with marinade.
4. Place chicken (skin side up) in cast iron or roasting pan and cook for 10–15 minutes.
5. Baste and roast for another 10–15 minutes. If skin is already well darkened, turn it over (if possible), baste again, and lower heat to 325°F.

6. Cook another few minutes, return to skin side facing up, and finish cooking until skin is super brown and crisp and chicken is cooked through. (The government would like that to be 165°F, but you can pull it before that if the juices from the chicken run clear, meaning that there's no sign of redness coming through.) Let it rest for 10–15 minutes.

Note: All times are approximate but whole chicken will take the longest, butterflied will take less, and if using pieces only, those will cook the most quickly.

* Tamari has a darker color and richer flavor than common Chinese soy sauce. Good ones have a thicker body and a sweetish, smoky, meaty flavor.

CRISPY DRY RUBBED CHICKEN THIGHS (INTUITIVE)

I have a thing for chicken thighs and a love affair with Costco, which sells them by the 32-pack. The good news is that they're incredibly easy to prepare and pretty hard to screw up, which makes them an ideal playground for experimenting with your gustatory intuition. I always prefer bone-in and skin-on for the best flavor, and obviously the crispy skin, but you could opt for the boneless and skinless if you prefer. If so, you should know that they cook more quickly and they shrink a whole bunch during cooking.

You simply flavor them, amp up the heat in the oven, and let it fly . . . so to speak. In fact, if all you put on the chicken was a nice hit of salt and pepper, and let it roast until super brown and crispy, they'd be plenty good. Yet there's so much more you can do to bring the flavor. That's where the "intuitive" part comes into play. By playing with different seasoning combinations—or what chefs call "flavor profiles"—you can create unlimited varieties of wonderful taste sensations. For example, if I feel like a Mexican or Southwestern flavor I make a Latin spice blend that's equal parts of chili powder, ancho chili powder, smoked paprika (*pimentón*), and kosher salt. If I want it spicy instead I'll douse the thighs with hot sauce. (I use Frank's because it already has plenty of salt in it.) Feeling like Asian? I might use soy sauce, fresh ginger, five-spice powder, maybe Sichuan peppercorns. For Italian, I'd use garlic, oregano, maybe some red wine vinegar. It's worth noting here that if you do use liquids for flavoring it can be slightly more challenging to get the intensely crisp skin that makes these thighs so irresistible. In that case, what I do is roast the thighs first for 15–20 minutes until they start to take on color, and then I'll baste them heavily with the liquid-based flavoring. Or if I'm using only a dry rub I'll cook them until crispy and apply a drizzle of honey or pomegranate molasses for those last few minutes of cooking. However, if you intend to fire them up over the grill, then go ahead and pour on the liquid flavoring up front . . . and baste along the way.

In any case, the point is that it's your opportunity to play, to create your own palette of flavorings, and your own go-to chicken dish. (Also works with turkey thighs, although roasting time will be longer.)

SERVES 4

INGREDIENTS
8 SKIN-ON, BONE-IN CHICKEN THIGHS
4 TEASPOONS DRY RUB (EQUAL PARTS OF CHILI POWDER, ANCHO CHILI POWDER, SMOKED PAPRIKA
    [PIMENTÓN], AND KOSHER SALT)

PREPARATION

1. Preheat oven to 475°F. Season both sides of chicken well with the dry rub. Roast on baking sheet skin side up for about 15 minutes, turn over and keep cooking for another 15 minutes. (Or not. This is one of those where you could keep it skin side for

the entire cooking time if the skin isn't burning. In either case, just make sure that the skin gets nice and brown and very crispy. That's where the action is.)

2. You can reduce heat at any point you see too much color on the chicken, or when your smoke alarm goes off. After 30 minutes, check for doneness. Your best bet is always the thermometer, where 165°F is your goal here, but you could also cut into the thigh, close to the bone, to ensure that there's no pinkness. If more cooking time is needed, return to skin side up and cook until skin is well browned and crispy and the meat is cooked through. Total cooking time can vary between 30–50 minutes depending on the size of the thighs and the heat of your oven.

3. You'll be tempted to dig right in, but let them sit and rest a few minutes before doing so. They're also good cold the next day.

Here's another spice blend alternative you could try; it's the creole dry rub that Emeril Lagasse famously called Emeril's Essence.

2½ TABLESPOONS PAPRIKA	1 TABLESPOON ONION POWDER
2 TABLESPOONS SALT	1 TABLESPOON CAYENNE PEPPER
2 TABLESPOONS GARLIC POWDER	1 TABLESPOON DRIED OREGANO
1 TABLESPOON BLACK PEPPER	1 TABLESPOON DRIED THYME

CHICKEN, KALE, AND PEPPERS

Kale is rarely better than when it's flavored by chicken and the sweet but mild heat from cubanelle or Italian frying peppers. A one-pot meal for four that brings a bit of excitement to the usual chicken dinner.

SERVES 4

INGREDIENTS
8 CHICKEN THIGHS (BEST ON THE BONE WITH SKIN)
SALT AND PEPPER
1 TABLESPOON OLIVE OIL
1 MEDIUM ONION, SLICED
4 CUBANELLE OR ITALIAN FRYING PEPPERS, SLICED
   IN RINGS
4 CLOVES GARLIC, PEELED
2 BUNCHES KALE, RINSED AND ROUGHLY CHOPPED
½–1 CUP WATER OR CHICKEN STOCK
ZEST OF 1 LEMON

PREPARATION

1. Preheat oven to 400°F and put a Dutch oven over medium heat while you season the chicken well with salt and pepper.

2. Heat up the oil in the Dutch oven and proceed to brown the chicken thighs well on both sides. Remove them, and add in the onions, peppers, and garlic. Hit 'em with a pinch of salt and stir them around for three or four minutes until softened and fragrant.

3. Place the kale in, sprinkle with a little salt and pepper, add ½ cup of water or stock, and bring up to a simmer. Then settle the chicken on top, skin side up, and insert into the oven, without a lid, cooking until chicken is browned and cooked through, around 20 minutes. Check after 10 minutes or so to make sure there's still some liquid remaining, or add a touch more. When ready, top it off with lemon zest.

ROAST TURKEY BREAST

People look forward to their Thanksgiving turkey. So why do so few folks make it the other 364 days of the year? I imagine it's because we see it as a cumbersome operation, appropriate only for a large gathering. But it doesn't have to be, especially if you make the breast only. Follow these four easy steps and I promise you a terrific tasting turkey that you'll be thankful for any day of the week. The key is to keep the white meat moist . . . so take the temperature, pull it out at 160 degrees, and let there be rest!

SERVES 6 PEOPLE, AND YOU MIGHT LEAVE LEFTOVERS FOR TOMORROW'S SANDWICH IF YOU'RE LUCKY

INGREDIENTS
2 CARROTS, CHOPPED
2 STALKS CELERY, CHOPPED
1 MEDIUM ONION, CHOPPED
2 TEASPOONS SALT
1 TEASPOON PEPPER
1 WHOLE BONE-IN FRESH TURKEY BREAST
   (AROUND 5 POUNDS)

OPTIONAL: 1 TABLESPOON FRESH CHOPPED ROSEMARY, SAGE, OR TARRAGON, OR 1 TEASPOON CHOPPED FRESH THYME

PREPARATION

1. Preheat oven to 425°F.

2. Spread chopped carrots, celery, and onions into roasting pan and season with a little of the salt and pepper (saving the majority of it for the turkey itself). Now season the turkey breast on both sides with the salt and pepper and drop it on top of veggies. (Drop it gently, otherwise carrots will go flying.) Feel free to sprinkle the pan with your favorite dried herbs (like rosemary, sage, thyme, or tarragon).

3. Roast turkey in oven, covering with aluminum foil if/when skin starts to get too crisp. Roasting time depends on size of the breast, and your oven; 5 pounds could take about 75 minutes. The surefire method is to cook to 160°F (an instant-read thermometer is a most worthwhile investment if you don't already own one) and then remove breast to a platter or serving plate.

4. While you allow the turkey to "rest" for 20–30 minutes, add a cup of water to the vegetables in pan. Over low flame, stir it around, making sure to scrape up any brown goodness that has adhered to the pan. Taste and adjust the sauce for seasoning. Slice turkey and serve with pan juices (jus) spooned over.

LET'S TALK TURKEY . . . BURGERS (WITH ONIONS AND DILL)

I can't be the only one who appreciates a good turkey burger. The problem is that they are often rightfully maligned for being dry and bland. That is easily rectified by amping up the flavor profile and adding a measure of moistness to ensure that you end with one that's tasty and juicy.

The flavor part is not too difficult because you can incorporate a wide variety of ingredients to the ground turkey before you make patties and cook 'em up. Variations aplenty include using your favorite spices or herbs—anything from a good hit of fresh rosemary or dried tarragon to cumin, curry, chili powder, toasted fennel seeds, seasoned salt, or soy sauce and a dash of sesame oil for an Asian accent. Use your imagination to customize.

As far as the moisture quotient, I quickly sauté onion until soft and fragrant and add it to the ground meat along with some freshly chopped dill, salt, and pepper. Then I cook 'em up until golden in either a frying pan/skillet or on the grill. The onions and dill keep them from getting dried out and contribute a wonderful flavor.

MAKES 4 BURGERS

INGREDIENTS
1½ TABLESPOONS OLIVE OIL
¼ CUP DICED ONION
1 POUND GROUND TURKEY (ORGANIC, IF POSSIBLE, AND NOT TOO LEAN)
¼ TEASPOON EACH OF SALT AND PEPPER
1 HANDFUL FRESH DILL, FINELY CHOPPED (ABOUT 3 TABLESPOONS)

PREPARATION

1. Heat 1 tablespoon of oil in skillet and sauté onions over medium heat until they're soft, fragrant, and just beginning to lightly brown.

2. Remove from pan and let them cool.

3. Mix the turkey in a bowl with onions, salt, pepper, and dill and form into four equal size hamburger patties.

4. Heat skillet with remaining ½ tablespoon of oil and cook hamburgers on medium high heat, turning once, until browned and cooked through, approximately 8 minutes. Perhaps instead of ketchup consider topping it with cranberry sauce (recipe page 204).

GAME DAY TURKEY MEATBALLS

Same story: gotta amp up the taste factor to end up with balls worth savoring. Simple: mount with onion, garlic, and salty cheese . . . followed by a long, hot bath in tomato sauce. They're good, real good.

MAKES ABOUT 20 ONE-BITE BALLS, SO DINNER FOR FOUR, OR APPS FOR 6

INGREDIENTS

1 POUND GROUND TURKEY (ORGANIC, IF POSSIBLE, AND NOT TOO LEAN)
⅓ CUP FINELY CHOPPED ONION
1 CLOVE GARLIC, FINELY MINCED
½ CUP GRATED PECORINO CHEESE (YES, PARMESAN IS FINE, TOO)
1 TEASPOON SALT
1 TABLESPOON OIL
2 CUPS TOMATO SAUCE (RECIPE PAGE 149)

PREPARATION

1. Using your hands, blend turkey together with onion, garlic, cheese, and salt in a large bowl. Spoon it out—literally, with a tablespoon, and gently form into balls with your hands. Or better yet, it's even more efficient and less messy if you have one of those mini ice cream scoopers so you can scoop and drop them directly into the waiting pan without having to use your hands at all to form them.

2. Heat oil in a large skillet until simmering, add balls, and brown them *well* on all sides. They're delicate, so don't handle them too much, but shake the pan periodically to get even browning.

3. Then plop them into a pot of simmering tomato sauce for half an hour. Not only will they benefit from the sauce, the sauce will benefit from them.

4. Straight up, inside Italian bread, over pasta or polenta . . . enjoy!

Red Meat, Pig, and Poultry (It's all good in small doses)

LOVE ME TENDER LOIN OF PORK

Ah, the tenderloin of pork. So lovely. Not hard to cook. But, as lean as skinless chicken breasts, it needs a little help to ensure that it becomes tasty and juicy rather than, well, tasteless and dry. Therefore, we'll brine it first, then maximize its flavor potential by applying the salty seasoning mix of your choosing (another "intuitive" play) and make sure not to overcook it. You want to see some pink inside. As for the seasoning, as long as you use salt, you can create the rest on your own.

To cook, you could go all "top of stove" in a heavy gauge pan (like cast-iron), or roasted in the oven. Or do both—whereby you'd sear it atop the stove and finish the cooking in the oven. I actually prefer that method because it produces a superior outside crusting and luscious light pinkness within. (You'll need an ovenproof pan.)

The key is your internal temperature. Well, not *your* internal temperature, the pork's. Anyway, you're going to want it somewhere in the vicinity of 145°F for medium rare and 160°F for medium. That means you're going to have to pull it from the heat 5 degrees *before* it reaches that temperature because it will continue cooking off the heat (residual cooking). You must also *let it rest* before cutting.

SERVES 2–3

INGREDIENTS

For the brine
20 OUNCES WATER (2½ CUPS)
1 OUNCE KOSHER SALT (ABOUT 2 TABLESPOONS)
1 OUNCE SUGAR (LIGHT BROWN IS IDEAL, BUT REGULAR CAN BE USED)
1 TABLESPOON BLACK PEPPERCORNS, CRUSHED OR FRESHLY GRATED
5 CLOVES GARLIC, ROUGHLY CHOPPED

OPTIONAL: 1½ TEASPOONS *herbes de Provence* (CAN SUBSTITUTE THYME AND/OR SAGE OR OTHER DRIED HERBS)

For the pork
1 POUND BONELESS PORK LOIN AT ROOM TEMPERATURE
2 TEASPOONS OIL FOR RUBBING
½–1 TEASPOON SEASONED SALT MIX (I COMBINE A TEASPOON OF SALT WITH A HALF TEASPOON EACH OF DRIED ROSEMARY, THYME, GARLIC POWDER, AND FRESHLY GROUND BLACK PEPPER. THAT'S MAKES MORE THAN YOU'LL NEED, BTW, SO YOU'LL HAVE SOME LEFT OVER FOR ANOTHER USE.)

Place the pork in the brining liquid, cover, and refrigerate for anywhere from a couple of hours to overnight. When ready to cook, make sure to dry the pork loin thoroughly.

PREPARATION

1. Preheat oven to 375°F.

2. Rub the loin with 1 teaspoon of oil and apply the salt mix all over.

3. Over high heat put a teaspoon of oil in ovenproof pan and sear meat well on both sides.

4. Place pan in oven and continue cooking until reaching the desired doneness/temperature, approximately 15–20 minutes.

5. Remove to cutting board, cover, and let it rest for 10 minutes, then slice and be happy.

Brining

Tasty and tender is what you get when you brine, the process of soaking food in a saltwater solution that is often infused with other savory flavors as well. This saline bath moisturizes meats and poultry, and adding aromatics will impart a piquant dimension. It works particularly well for pork loin, which can become somewhat dried out when cooked. The basic ratio for a brining liquid is 20 parts of water to one salt, to which I then might add aromatics, pepper, herbs, and sugar.

BRAISED PORK "RIBS" MOLE-STYLE

This is as succulent, saucy, and satisfying as it gets. A one-pot affair that uses an inexpensive cut of meat slowly braised beyond tender in a flavor-filled broth of beer suffused with Latin spices, this dish is great for a crowd. It is not a *mole* by any means, which is a rich and complex Mexican sauce that typically requires MANY ingredients to make. Rather, it is an attempt to create a robust braising medium that incorporates a few of the flavorings one might find in a mole, such as chile peppers and cocoa. They key here is to brown all the meat well without burning the brown material (*sucs*) that will be accruing in the bottom of the pot. Again, heat management matters.

Notes:
Costco sells these Pork Shoulder Country Style Ribs Boneless. I don't recall seeing them elsewhere. Don't fret if you can't find them, though; there are options. You can either get them on the bone or you can buy pork shoulder—with or without the bone—and use the same basic ingredients and technique.

Although you could purchase something like Goya Adobo or Sazón in the supermarket, I'd suggest that you just as easily make a Latin spice mix yourself. (If you do store-bought, make sure to add some chili powder for flavor and color.) I blend chili powder, ancho chile powder, smoked paprika, and salt. You can also add or substitute cumin, oregano, and chipotle chile powder, which contributes another smoky element. And you could just as easily use three or four whole dried chiles (e.g., ancho, chipotle, pasilla, etc.), which I actually toss directly into the broth. They'll break apart over time; just remember to remove their stems either before or after cooking. They are a bitch to discover by accident in your mouth.

SERVES 6–8

INGREDIENTS

1 TABLESPOON OIL

4 TABLESPOONS LATIN SPICE MIX (ONE TABLESPOON EACH OF CHILI POWDER, ANCHO CHILI POWDER, SMOKED PAPRIKA, AND SALT)

3–3½ POUNDS PORK SHOULDER "COUNTRY STYLE RIBS BONELESS"

1 MEDIUM ONION, CHOPPED

8 CLOVES GARLIC, PEELED AND CRUSHED

1½–2 BOTTLES OF FULL-BODIED BEER

¼ CUP KETCHUP

2 TABLESPOONS BROWN SUGAR

1 TABLESPOON UNSWEETENED COCOA POWDER

¼ TEASPOON CINNAMON

Red Meat, Pig, and Poultry (It's all good in small doses)

PREPARATION

1. While you heat oil in a large, heavy pot (like a Dutch oven), spread about ¾ of the spice mix all over and around the meat. (Reserve some for later in the cooking.)

2. Brown the seasoned meat well on both sides, being careful not to burn the bits forming on the pan's bottom. When all browned, drop in the onion and garlic and move them around until you smell them cooking.

Note: You could remove the meat to sauté the garlic and onion for a few moments until fragrant, but it's an avoidable extra step if you can instead reposition the meat so that the "aromatics" are exposed to the bottom of the pan.

3. Dump* in the beer—reserving a swig for yourself—to cover ¾ of the meat. Now the ketchup, brown sugar, cocoa, and cinnamon go in, as well as the remaining spice mix IF you want a lotta flavor in there. Bring it to a boil, then reduce to simmer for a long while, 2–3 hours. You don't have to worry about it falling off the bone because there is no bone. However, after two hours, the meat generally maintains some semblance of shape, whereas after three hours of cooking, it falls to pieces faster than Patsy Cline. (I'll admit, that's a pretty obscure reference.) In that case, it becomes more like a chunky pork stew . . . and works quite well served over pretty much anything or inside some warm tortillas, perhaps touched up with some avocado, shredded cheese, cilantro, and salsa or green sauce. How good does that sound?

* I do recognize that *dump* is neither typical culinary terminology, nor particularly taste appealing.

CHAPTER NINE

ADVENTURES IN SEAFOOD

FISH IN FOIL
(POISSON EN PAPILLOTE PROVENÇALE)

This is a foolproof steamed fish recipe, which will no doubt showcase your culinary genius. Wouldn't it impress your guests at dinner if you served an elegant entrée of *rouget en papillote? En papillote* is a French cooking term meaning to wrap in parchment paper or tinfoil. Unveiling these beautifully presented pouches reveals aromas reminiscent of Provençal cooking such as freshly picked tarragon, oil-cured Niçoise olives (pitted or not, your choice!), sweet cherry tomatoes, and orange zest. Serve over rice or steamed baby potatoes to soak up the fragrant juices.

MAKES 2 SERVINGS

INGREDIENTS
2 1-INCH THICK, 8-OUNCE RED SNAPPER FILLETS, SKINNED
SALT AND FRESHLY GROUND BLACK PEPPER
6 GRAPE OR CHERRY TOMATOES, CUT IN HALF
6 BLACK OLIVES, PITTED (OR NOT) AND SLICED (OR NOT)
¼ TEASPOON RED PEPPER FLAKES (OPTIONAL)
2 TEASPOONS UNSALTED BUTTER, CUT INTO BITS
½ TEASPOON ORANGE ZEST
4 SPRIGS FRESH HERBS, SUCH AS THYME OR TARRAGON

PREPARATION

1. Crack open a bottle of Sancerre or Pinot Gris. Have a sip. (Optional step, but recommended.)

2. Put a rack in the middle of the oven, and preheat oven to 500°F.

3. Cut two large (about 12-by-15-inch) sheets of parchment paper (or foil). Fold each sheet in half lengthwise to crease, then unfold. Season fish with salt and pepper and place one fillet to the right of the crease on each sheet. Top each fillet with 6 tomato halves, half of the olives, ⅛ teaspoon red pepper flakes, half each of butter and zest, and 2 herb sprigs. (If you followed step 1, drop a splash of white wine into the package.)

4. Fold parchment paper back over the fillet at the crease. Then, starting at the top, left corner, encase the fillets by folding the parchment over in triangles, overlapping successive folds and moving in a semicircular path around the fish. Smooth out the folds as you go and tuck in the last fold to completely seal the *papillote*.

5. Heat a large baking sheet in the oven for 5 minutes. Position the papillotes on the hot baking sheet and bake for 9 minutes.

6. To serve, transfer each packet to a plate. Use a knife to slit the top of each packet and open to fully expose the fish, being careful not to burn your fingers as the steam escapes. Slide each fillet and the accompanying sauce onto a plate, discarding the parchment. Receive applause.

SEARED TUNA WRAP WITH MANGO CHUTNEY

This quick and easy-to-make seared tuna wrap is a way to bring various ethnic food flavors together in a single dish. Japanese sushi-grade tuna, cooked until crisp on the outside and raw on the inside, is paired with Mexican tortillas, and enhanced with Indian mango chutney. Incorporating sweet, salty, and spicy flavor notes, this vibrant and healthful wrap makes for a perfect lunch or an appetizer for a more elaborate dinner party. Sliced into bite-size portions, the wrap can also be served as a "happy hour" finger food.

Note: Stonewall Kitchen makes a delicious mango chutney, but feel free to use other brands.

MAKES 2 WRAPS

INGREDIENTS
8 OUNCES SUSHI-GRADE TUNA
SALT AND FRESHLY GROUND PEPPER TO TASTE
1 TEASPOON PEANUT OR NEUTRAL (LIKE GRAPESEED) OIL
2 8-INCH TORTILLAS
2 TEASPOONS MANGO CHUTNEY
1 TABLESPOON FRESHLY CHOPPED CILANTRO
½ LIME, CUT INTO 4 EQUAL PIECES
DASH OF TABASCO (OPTIONAL)

PREPARATION

1. Season the tuna with salt and pepper to taste.

2. In a small sauté pan, heat the oil over high heat. Sear the tuna until crisp on the outside, about 1 minute or so per side. Transfer the tuna to a cutting board and slice into ½-inch thick slices.

3. Place a tortilla on open flame until lightly charred, about 5–10 seconds per side. Repeat with second tortilla. Divide the tuna between the two tortillas. Top each with half the chutney and cilantro. Squeeze a lime wedge, and if using, some Tabasco, over the whole thing. Roll the tortillas to enclose the filling. Halve on the bias and serve. (The one place where bias is good.)

FILET OF SOLE À LA MEUNIÉRE

This is a classic French preparation of fish with a lemon butter sauce. It's hard not to like, yet pretty simple to make. It is also kind of elegant and somewhat marvelous, which makes it a good option to serve for a small dinner party, especially when you have access to fresh fish. And a nice bottle of sauvignon blanc.

MAKES 4 SERVINGS

INGREDIENTS

4 8-OUNCE PIECES OF FILET OF SOLE (CAN ALSO
 USE LEMON OR GREY SOLE OR ANOTHER FLAKY
 WHITE FISH)
SALT AND PEPPER
FLOUR FOR DREDGING
2–3 TABLESPOONS CLARIFIED BUTTER OR OLIVE OIL
1 LEMON, JUICED
4 TABLESPOONS UNSALTED BUTTER
HANDFUL OF PARSLEY, FINELY CHOPPED

PREPARATION

1. Season fish with salt and pepper, dredge filets in flour, and wipe off excess.

2. In a large sauté pan, warm the clarified butter (or oil) over medium high heat. When it's hot, add the fish and cook until lightly golden brown, about 2–3 minutes per side. Remove fish and set aside.

3. Make beurre noisette (see recipe on page 196). Either pour the lemon juice directly over the filets and then top with brown butter. OR . . . stir the lemon juice directly into the butter, in which case it will bubble and splatter and make a small commotion, which I kind of like. So cool the butter a bit before adding lemon juice. Garnish with parsley.

CLAMS WITH CHORIZO (PORK AND CLAMS)

In planning a trip to Portugal I was most excited about finding and devouring clams with pork, a classic combination in Portuguese cooking. In my version, I combine small littleneck clams with Spanish chorizo (already cured, not uncooked), which lends a smoky counterpoint to the tangy dry white wine–flavored broth in which the clams are steamed open. It is an easy, yet impressive, start to any meal. It also makes for a complete meal when served with a simple salad. As for wine, the rule is never to cook with any wine you wouldn't drink, but I'd even take it a step further: cook these clams with the very wine that you are going to drink. I'd suggest a nice Sancerre or Pinot Gris.

Note: Clams should be individually scrubbed under cold running water or rinsed in three changes of water to get rid of any sand.

MAKES 4 APPETIZER PORTIONS

INGREDIENTS
1 TABLESPOON OLIVE OIL
½ MEDIUM ONION, FINELY DICED
3 CLOVES GARLIC PEELED, FINELY SLICED
½ CUP DICED (BITE-SIZE) SPANISH CHORIZO
2 DOZEN LITTLENECK CLAMS, CLEANED
2 CUPS WHITE WINE, LIKE SANCERRE OR PINOT GRIS
1 TEASPOON BUTTER
SALT AND PEPPER TO TASTE
HANDFUL CHOPPED PARSLEY, FOR GARNISH

PREPARATION

1. Heat the oil in a large sauté pan over medium heat, and sauté the onion, garlic, and chorizo, stirring until the onions are translucent and chorizo renders some of its fat, 3 to 4 minutes.

2. Add the clams to the pan, pour in wine, cover, and simmer until clams open, 5 to 6 minutes.

3. Place pan contents except broth in serving bowl, discarding any unopened clams.

4. Reduce the remaining broth over high heat to about 1 cup.

5. Season with salt and pepper, add the butter, stirring it until just melted, and drizzle over the clams.

6. Garnish with parsley and serve with crusty bread on the side.

9 Ways to Satisfy a Clam Frenzy

It started with nibbling, munching, even licking every clam I could get my tongue on.

It was coastal Maine, America's very own heartland of clam, and I was on a clam bender.

In the midst of my mollusk frenzy, I took a moment to post an image to Facebook. It was of a large bucket of steamers. I was taken aback by the rapid response of my friend Julie, who commented, "Am I the only one who thinks clams are disgusting?"

No, she is undoubtedly not the only clam hater. So why was I so surprised? Because Julie is an Ivy League-educated, supremely gifted artist, and an otherwise lovely, open-minded soul . . . *with a profound appreciation for the sea.*

Therefore, I feel a responsibility to report on all the clammy wonderfulness that Julie is missing as a consequence of her inexplicable and wrongheaded aversion.

Fried clams. If there are three perfect fried foods in the world, the other two are chicken and potatoes. In the case of the clam, that is due to the textural sensation of the golden coating juxtaposed against the salty sweetness of the entrapped clam. However, *caveat emptor*: there are fried clams, and then there are fried clams. More specifically, fried clam strips, which use only a portion of the whole clam, yield an unworthy breading-to-clam ratio. Instead, what you want is the whole clam belly, well coated and properly fried in clean, hot oil, to produce the total joy that comes from the soft, seaworthy oozing revealed upon mastication. A squeeze of lemon is fine, and perhaps a tiny dip of homemade tartar sauce might enhance the heavenly happiness. But none for Julie.

Steamed clams. Here I refer to the soft-shell bivalves known as "steamers." Best when served in the aforementioned bucket, they do require a little work before ingestion. That is, one must perform somewhat of a culinary circumcision by pulling off the small, black foreskin-like membrane that covers the neck of the clam. Don't be put off by this quick and easy procedure, for when these plump-from-the-sea sand dwellers are good and fresh, they want for nothing more than the briefest bath in the hot clam broth that accompanies their arrival for the purpose of removing any extraneous sand particles. Sure, you could also dip 'em into the warm melted butter, but when their succulent, bulbous bellies are at their eating peak, they're so sweet that you shouldn't even have to. And Julie don't get none.

Baked clams. A.k.a. *Clams Oreganata* and *Clams Casino*. Some places will chop up clams and fill a large clam shell with a little clam and a lot of superfluous breading. Don't go to those places. The experience you're paying for is the whole clam, its own half-shell stuffed with fresh, seasoned bread crumbs, then placed under a burning hot broiler so as to render it browned and just crisp enough. Then, one sucks out the entire production at once, creating a cacophonous culinary crescendo of clam and crumb in your watering mouth. A proper baked clam is a thing of beauty—sweet, salty, crunchy, and a little chewy. Clams casino, by the way, include a little bit of bacon, adding another flavorful dimension to an already wondrous composition. Disgusting? *Au contraire*, Julie.

Clam chowder. You've got your creamy New England variety and your tomato-based Manhattan version. Each has its proponents and detractors.

Although neither will hurt you, if I had to choose only one to warm the cockles of my heart on a dreary, damp, rainy day, it would have to be New England's. Chock-full of moist potatoes and generous, fat chunks of quahog clams peeking out from a rich, velvety clam broth, often accented by the slightly smoky hint of bacon. Sorry, Julie, only tomato soup for you.

Clam pizza. They may not be too common to come by, but if you like clams, come by one. The clam pizza at Zuppardi's in West Haven, Connecticut, for example, is made with just-shucked clams and a hint of fresh garlic on a perfectly blistered pizza crust. There is no cheese on this pie, nor tomato sauce. Rather, imagine something akin to a paper thin, piping hot bruschetta topped with gossamer clams and a sauce produced by the very liquid they release upon baking. Say what you might about clam pie; this is a work of gastronomic art. I've also had it with mozzarella and it is none too shabby. Alas, Julie won't be having a slice.

Linguini with clam sauce. Nor will Julie be enjoying a perfect plate of *al dente* pasta populated by whole baby clams, aroused by garlic, swimming ever so lightly in a shallow pool of goodness produced by olive oil with perhaps a hit of butter that has been suffused by the juicy juice of the clams themselves. On behalf of all Americans—with the exception of Julie—I'd like to thank the Italians for this elegant contribution to civilization.

Clams in black bean sauce. Let us not leave out the Chinese when it comes to plaudits for excellent clam combinations. In this formidable pairing, one licks the clam from the shell and immediately notices its natural sweetness when set against the pungent black sauce. Julie will have to make do with the white rice on the side.

Raw clams. Served "on the half shell," this is pleasure of the pristine variety. Although *littlenecks* have come to stand for a size categorization, their name is said to have derived from the source where they were originally cultivated, Little Neck Bay, in Queens, New York, where I coincidentally fell for my first love, Gina Maria Imbriola Theresa Camiletti. My second love: clams. Or, you might opt for the *cherrystones*, which are larger, thicker and chewier, but also delightful. In either case, they require nothing more than a light squirt of lemon and a touch of horseradish-studded cocktail sauce with perhaps a splash of Tabasco if you so desire. But please, not too much; it's the clam you're paying for, not the sauce. And what you get for your money is a symphony of slurping the sweet, saline essence of the sea. One must appreciate the natural goodness of a food with so much flavor, yet so little fat, carbs, or calories. Clams 8, Julie 0.

Grilled clams. Whole, rinsed, unopened clams are placed onto the grate of a hot barbecue, the grill covered. Almost miraculously, they will open themselves the second they are ready, about 4–5 minutes, depending on the heat of the grill and size of the clam. Once they do, you will remove them ever so gently so as not to lose one single eyedropful of the glorious liquid inside the shell—officially known as the clam's liquor—in which they have just steamed. You will proceed to vacuum out the entire clam and its intoxicating broth into your awaiting gullet and marvel at the wonder of one of the very few foods in existence that require *not one single other ingredient* to improve upon it. For my money, this is the very best one-ingredient dish in the world. Your friends will ask for the recipe, and you will think kindly of me. Except, of course, for Julie.

SCALLOPS PROVENÇAL

Another seemingly fancy-sounding dish that you can do well with ease and in not a ton of time. The trick again is knowing when to stop cooking the scallops. Like shrimp, they can go from pretty perfect to pretty chewy in no time flat. That said, you might try practicing on a single scallop to get a sense of how long you need to cook it. Not to complicate it, but of course not all sea scallops (the bigger ones vs. the smaller bay scallops) are the same size. In every case, what you're looking for is what is called *just cooked through,* which means they do not look raw on the inside, but they don't look well done either. There is a middle ground, and that's what you want—a slight hint of translucence. The rest of the cooking process is super simple. The finished product is sublime.

Note: If you care to bring an extra dimension to this, you might consider that red pepper puree/coulis on page 198, served either on the side or underneath.

SERVES 2

INGREDIENTS
3 TABLESPOONS OLIVE OIL
1 POUND LARGE SEA SCALLOPS, PATTED DRY
2 GARLIC CLOVES, SLICED THIN
1 MEDIUM TOMATO, DICED
⅛ TEASPOON DRIED THYME, CRUMBLED (CAN
    SUBSTITUTE WITH ¼ TEASPOON FRESH)
¼ CUP SHREDDED FRESH BASIL LEAVES

PREPARATION

1. In a pan wide enough to cook the scallops in one layer, heat half of the oil over *high heat* until it's hot and sear the scallops for 1 to 2 minutes on each side, or until they are browned and *just cooked through*.

2. Set the scallops aside on a plate and keep them warm by covering with foil.

3. Add the remaining half of the oil to the pan and cook the garlic over moderate heat, stirring for a minute or so until it turns light golden.

4. Add the tomato and the thyme and stir the mixture around for 1 minute.

5. Season with salt and pepper, spoon it over and around the scallops, then top it off with the basil.

MUSSELS MARINIÈRE (IN WHITE WINE)

Something magical happens when shellfish release their natural saline juices into a winey broth infused with herbs, aromatics, and a touch of butter. Once you master this recipe, you're going to want to make it frequently. Great for an appetizer or fine for dinner, too. Just make sure you have a baguette on hand to sop up all that luscious broth in the bowl. And a lot of napkins.

ENOUGH FOR 4 AS MAIN COURSE OR 6 AS AN APPETIZER.

INGREDIENTS
4 DOZEN MUSSELS
2 CUPS DRY WHITE WINE
½ CUP SHALLOTS, MINCED
½ CUP MINCED PARSLEY
BAY LEAF
3 SPRIGS FRESH THYME (CAN SUBSTITUTE 1
    TABLESPOON DRY)
1–2 TABLESPOONS UNSALTED BUTTER

PREPARATION

1. Clean the mussels by scrubbing them well under running water, removing anything attached to or coming from inside the shell. Tap any that are open and throw them away if they don't close. Rinse again.

2. Place all the ingredients except for the mussels and butter into a large pot and bring to a boil. Then reduce heat and simmer, covered, for 2 minutes. Now add the mussels, cover, and return heat to high. As soon as the mussels open, which usually takes about 3 to 4 minutes, they're ready; remove them with a slotted spoon to one large bowl, or multiple small bowls.

3. Stir the butter into the cooking liquid until incorporated. Taste for seasoning. Ladle liquid over mussels and serve immediately. Pass the baguette.

ANCHO CHILE SHRIMP (INTUITIVE)

This dish is a Short Order Dad staple in our home. If you love shrimp—or you see it on sale—try it this way. The beauty of ancho chile is that it imparts a faint fruity smokiness, not heat. And the dish is very adaptable: we eat them straight up, as an appetizer, or serve them over a bed of linguine as a first or main course. Or remove the tail altogether, slice the shrimp in half, and place them inside a couple of tortillas with melty cheese and a touch of salsa, toast both sides, and you've got yourself a killer quesadilla. In which case, don't forget a margarita for the grown-ups (on page 241).

Note: The trick with shrimp is not overcooking them. They become rubbery when you do.

INGREDIENTS

1 POUND LARGE SHRIMP, PREFERABLY WILD, PEELED AND DEVEINED

2 TABLESPOONS ANCHO CHILE POWDER (USE REGULAR CHILI POWDER IF YOU CAN'T FIND ANCHO, BUT TRY TO FIND THE ANCHO)

4 CLOVES GARLIC, PEELED AND THINLY SLICED

3 TABLESPOONS OLIVE OIL

SALT AND BLACK PEPPER TO TASTE

2 TABLESPOONS FRESH SQUEEZED LIME JUICE

LARGE HANDFUL FRESH CHOPPED CILANTRO (AROUND 3 TABLESPOONS)

PREPARATION

1. In a bowl, toss shrimp with ancho powder so that it is coated. Add garlic. This may be refrigerated, well covered, for several hours at this point.

2. When ready to cook, heat olive oil in large skillet over medium high heat. When oil begins to shimmer, add shrimp in one layer. Sprinkle with salt and pepper.

3. When shrimp turns from translucent to that lovely red color, turn over and cook on the other side until just about done. This will only take a few minutes. Add the lime juice and toss until completely cooked.

4. Remove to plate. Check and adjust seasonings, including lime, then top with cilantro, serve, and enjoy.

Ancho Shrimp over Fettuccini

If you decide to serve this over pasta you're going to need to use more oil and lime juice to serve as your sauce. So cook a pound of fettuccine, have more olive oil, lime juice, and cilantro available to dress the pasta, AND dice up a ripe avocado and toss that in as well. Good stuff.

CHAPTER TEN

SUPERBOWLS—NOODLES, SOUPS, AND SALADS

DIY TOMATO SAUCE

Make your own. Period. I cannot recall the last time I purchased tomato sauce in a jar from a supermarket. Maybe a thousand years ago. Why? Making your own is fresher, less expensive, pretty easy, and better. And all you basically need is oil, onions, garlic, and decent tomatoes that are perfectly good from a can. This recipe probably makes more than you need for a typical meal, but it freezes well and will come in handy not only for pasta, but for my chicken parmigiana (page 111) and meatball (page 123) recipes, too.

MAKES ABOUT 6 CUPS

INGREDIENTS
¼ CUP EXTRA-VIRGIN OLIVE OIL
¼ CUP ONION, FINELY CHOPPED
6 GARLIC CLOVES, PEELED AND THINLY SLICED
2 28-OUNCE CANS PEELED WHOLE TOMATOES,
   CRUSHED BY HAND AND JUICES RESERVED
1 TEASPOON SALT, OR TO TASTE
1 TEASPOON SUGAR (OPTIONAL), OR TO TASTE IF
   YOUR TOMATOES ARE TOO ACIDIC

PREPARATION

1. In a large saucepan, heat the olive oil over moderate heat.

2. Add the onion and garlic and stir occasionally until soft and light golden brown, about 6 to 8 minutes.

3. Add the tomatoes in their juice and salt, and bring to a boil.

4. Lower the heat and simmer for 30 minutes or so until sauce thickens, occasionally stirring and mashing tomatoes with a fork or potato masher. (In fact, you *should* blend it if you prefer smooth to chunky.)

5. Check seasoning and if sauce tastes too acidic, add sugar and cook a few minutes more.

This sauce is good for a week in the fridge, so you can easily make ahead, or keep it frozen airtight for up to 4 months in the freezer.

TURKEY MEAT SAUCE

I'm not here to convince you that turkey meat sauce is superior to the kind that's normally made with pork, beef, veal, and lamb. But you can make it taste really good without using meats. So there's that.

ENOUGH FOR A POUND OF PASTA

INGREDIENTS
1 TABLESPOON OLIVE OIL
1 POUND GROUND TURKEY (ORGANIC IF POSSIBLE, AND NOT TOO LEAN)
1 CARROT, CHOPPED
1 STALK CELERY, CHOPPED
1 MEDIUM ONION, CHOPPED
3 CLOVES GARLIC, PEELED AND MINCED
1 TEASPOON DRIED OREGANO
SALT AND PEPPER
1 28-OUNCE CAN WHOLE TOMATOES AND JUICE, CRUSHED BY HAND OR PULSED IN BLENDER (REMEMBER THE SAN MARZANOS, IF POSSIBLE)
PINCH NUTMEG (OPTIONAL)

PREPARATION

1. Heat olive oil in a large skillet over moderate heat and cook turkey, stirring and breaking up lumps, until just cooked through, about 3 minutes.

2. Transfer turkey to a bowl with a slotted spoon and in remaining fat in skillet cook chopped vegetables (carrot, celery, onion, and garlic) with oregano, and salt and pepper to taste, over moderate heat, stirring occasionally, until vegetables are just softened, about 4 minutes.

3. Stir in tomatoes and return the turkey with any juices in bowl.

4. Add nutmeg, if using.

5. Simmer for 15–20 minutes, adjust seasoning, and serve as is, or consider blending it for a smoother sauce.

CACIO E PEPE

(Spaghetti with Pecorino Romano and Black Pepper)

My kids didn't believe me about this one. As much as they adore pasta, they certainly didn't think they'd like one with *this much pepper*. Alas, it is their favorite pasta in the world. Brought to you by the Italians, the sauce in this classic Roman spaghetti dish is composed of Pecorino Romano cheese, a ton of crushed black pepper, and a bit of the pasta cooking water. My strong suggestion if you make it is to use imported Pecorino Romano (it's hard, aged, and salty) if you want the real deal.

To know: *al dente* literally means "to the bite," which means that pasta should be cooked to the point where it maintains a little chewiness. NOT soft and mushy. So in making this dish, and all pasta for that matter, taste your pasta while it cooks so that you can pull it from the water while it still has some "bite" to it.

SERVES 4 TO 6

INGREDIENTS
6 OUNCES PECORINO ROMANO CHEESE, FINELY
   GRATED (ABOUT 3 CUPS)
1 POUND SPAGHETTI, LINGUINE, OR BUCATINI
1½ TEASPOONS SALT
1 TABLESPOON EXTRA-VIRGIN OLIVE OIL
1½ TEASPOONS COARSELY GROUND BLACK PEPPER

PREPARATION

1. Put cheese in a large bowl. Put a pot of water on to boil. When boiling, add pasta and salt and cook, stirring frequently. When pasta is just *al dente,* remove it by either draining it into a colander set over a bowl OR by using tongs. Either way, **make sure to reserve 1½ cups of that cooking water!** Place drained pasta in a bowl.

2. Slowly whisk about a cup of your reserved cooking water into the grated Pecorino until smooth. Keep whisking as you add in oil and black pepper. Pour cheese mixture over pasta, and toss vigorously to coat all the pasta. You want the sauce to cling to the pasta and be creamy but not watery, so you can adjust the consistency with the remaining reserved pasta water.

3. Serve immediately, with additional Pecorino and pepper on the side.

PASTA WITH SQUASH

Cutting squash can be challenging because of its thick skin (unlike some people I know). But it's certainly doable. Alternatively, squash comes already peeled and cut in many supermarkets these days, so there's a ready excuse to go the lazy way. Roasting, as we know, makes the veg soft and sweet, and a delightful component of this toothsome* pasta dish.

Notes:
1) This sauce goes best with a tubular shaped pasta like penne, ziti, or rigatoni.
2) To convert this from a side dish to something more ample, you might add prosciutto at the end. Cooked pancetta would not hurt you, either.

SERVES 4

INGREDIENTS
1 POUND BUTTERNUT SQUASH
¼ CUP OLIVE OIL
SALT AND PEPPER
NUTMEG, FRESHLY GRATED
1 POUND PASTA
1 MEDIUM ONION, CHOPPED
2 CLOVES GARLIC, MINCED
1 CUP CHICKEN OR VEGETABLE STOCK
LARGE HANDFUL PARSLEY, CHOPPED (2–3
   TABLESPOONS)
¼ CUP PARMESAN CHEESE
RED PEPPER FLAKES (OPTIONAL)

PREPARATION

1. Preheat oven to 450°F.

2. Mix squash together with 2 tablespoons of the oil; sprinkle with salt, pepper, and nutmeg. Lay it flat on a baking sheet and roast until it's tender and beginning to brown, about 15–20 minutes.

3. Bring a large pot of water to the boil and add a good bit of salt. Cook pasta until *al dente*, drain it, *and save a cup of the cooking water.*

4. Meanwhile add remaining 2 tablespoons of oil to a pan over medium high heat and sauté onion and garlic for a couple of minutes until soft and just beginning to brown. Pour in the stock and bring mixture to simmer, then fold in the pasta, squash, parsley, cheese, and pepper flakes, if using. Stir to combine everything together. If sauce seems too thick you can add in some of the pasta cooking water, a little bit at a time. Adjust seasoning to taste. But really, you know that by now. Must I keep repeating myself?

*In writing this, I felt that the word *toothsome* was appropriate, but wasn't entirely sure what it meant. Hang on a minute, let me look it up. Okay, according to Google, here you go:

tooth·some ˈto͞oTHsəm/ adjective. (of food) temptingly tasty. "a toothsome morsel"

synonyms: tasty, delicious, luscious, mouthwatering, delectable, succulent;

More: tempting, appetizing, inviting; informal scrumptious, nummy, finger-licking, melt-in-your-mouth, lip-smacking, "a toothsome lemon tart"

Yeah, that's right.

RIGHTEOUS RISOTTO

This is the only time I will use this word in the book, but *yummy* seems to be the ideal description for this classic, creamy rice dish. To do it right, you should be willing to spend about fifteen minutes over the stove because in the ideal world you'd be adding stock gradually and incrementally to the rice as it is absorbed. But really, folks, let's be honest: the world is not ideal. SO . . . if you're feeling lazy and impatient (my default position) I suppose you could add the stock all at once and hope for the best results, but I can't guarantee you'll get them*. I'm not here to judge, just inform. What matters is that you get the right Italian rice, specifically intended for risotto. Arborio is the most common, but you might discover others. (Carnaroli, for example.) Also, you can find the end result in image form on page 102.

SERVES 4–6

INGREDIENTS
ABOUT 3½ CUPS UNSALTED CHICKEN STOCK
1 TABLESPOON OLIVE OIL
1 TABLESPOON UNSALTED BUTTER
¼ CUP FINELY CHOPPED ONION (OR SHALLOT)
1 CUP (8 OUNCES) ARBORIO-TYPE RICE (ITALIAN
    RICE, SMALL ROUND KERNELS)
½ TEASPOON SALT (AND PEPPER TO TASTE)
¼ CUP GRATED PARMESAN CHEESE

PREPARATION

1. Heat up the chicken stock in a pot over a low simmer.

2. Heat oil and melt butter in a skillet over medium high heat. When bubbling hot, add onion and sauté for a minute or so, until softened, not browned.

3. Add the rice and salt, stirring and toasting the rice until it takes on just a hint of golden color (2 minutes or so).

4. Spoon in one ladle of stock and stir around using a wooden spoon, until absorbed. Then add the next ladle and repeat the process until all the stock is absorbed. The rice should be creamy and tender at that point, probably around 12 minutes or so.

5. Take it off the heat, blend in the Parmesan cheese, taste and adjust seasoning, and serve at once. Notice smiles.

* An alternate way of doing this is to add 3 cups of the stock at the beginning, bring it to a simmer, cover the pot, and cook for about 10 minutes or so until most of the liquid has been absorbed. Then uncover and proceed as above, adding in that final bit of remaining stock and cooking before completing with cheese.

PEA SOUP (*POTAGE DE PETITS POIS*)

There is something a little luxurious about a pool of thick, steaming, bright-green soup set in a white bowl. And there's no reason to buy soup already prepared when you can so easily make a seriously scrumptious version yourself with minimal effort. Use frozen peas, which tend to keep their sweetness and vibrant color, even when frozen. The key to preparing this luscious and delightful first course is to gently "sweat" the carrot, celery, and onion base, and avoid "caramelizing," or browning altogether. When ready to serve this fragrant and colorful soup, don't just say pea soup. Instead, call it *potage de petits pois* (pronounced PO—Tä ZH duh petty pwah).

SERVES 2

INGREDIENTS
1 TABLESPOON OLIVE OIL
1 CARROT, FINELY DICED
1 STALK CELERY, FINELY DICED
1 MEDIUM ONION, FINELY DICED
1 CLOVE GARLIC, FINELY DICED
2 CUPS PEAS
4 CUPS BEST QUALITY CHICKEN BROTH
SALT AND PEPPER TO TASTE

OPTIONAL GARNISHES: FRESHLY MINCED TARRAGON, CROUTONS, OR CRÈME FRAÎCHE

PREPARATION

1. In a large saucepan over low heat place first five ingredients. "Sweat" the vegetable base until fragrant and onions are translucent, about 5 minutes.

2. Add peas, broth, salt, and pepper. Bring to a boil and then lower to simmer for about 20 minutes.

3. Turn off heat and blend to desired texture in blender or food processor. Top with optional garnishes if you wish.

WORLD-CLASS CHICKEN SOUP

This one requires a little prep work, but once you smell the aroma that fills your home as it simmers, I would ask that you think of me. (And then buy another copy of this book for a friend or family member, please.) The key, as always, is to get the best chicken you can. Take note that the onion, celery, and carrot in the ingredient list below will have two separate uses. Some of it goes into the initial cooking liquid to infuse the chicken broth, and then later in the process, the rest will go into the soup itself. Once you master this one, friends and family will flock. (Unlike this chicken, alas, which will no longer.) And it freezes very well, too, for that cold winter's day.

8 SERVINGS, AT LEAST

INGREDIENTS

1 3–3½ POUNDS BROILER CHICKEN, WHOLE (KOSHER OR ORGANIC IS BEST)

1 ONION, HALF CUT INTO LARGE PIECES, THE OTHER HALF CUT INTO SMALL DICE

3 CELERY STALKS, HALF CUT INTO LARGE CHUNKS, THE OTHER HALF CUT INTO SMALL DICE

3 CARROTS, 1 CUT INTO LARGE CHUNKS, THE OTHER 2 CUT INTO SMALL DICE

4–5 CLOVES WHOLE GARLIC, PEELED

1 BUNCH DILL, 2 BRANCHES LEFT WHOLE, THE REST REMOVED FROM BRANCHES AND FINELY CHOPPED

WATER

1 PARSNIP, CUT INTO SMALL DICE

1 TURNIP, CUT INTO SMALL DICE

1 LEEK, CUT INTO SMALL DICE

SALT AND PEPPER TO TASTE

FINELY CHOPPED PARSLEY AND OR/SCALLIONS (AS OPTIONAL/TOPPINGS, BUT UNNECESSARY IF YOU USE DILL)

PREPARATION

1. Remove all the skin from the chicken except for the wings. Clean and rinse the chicken well, inside and out.

2. In a large pot, lay the chicken with the large pieces of onion, celery, and carrots. Add the garlic cloves, the dill branches, and enough cold water to cover it all. Boil with lid on for about 45 minutes.

3. Remove the chicken as well as the rest of the ingredients with a slotted spoon. (Although you could certainly cut up and use these aromatic vegetables, their flavor has already been well absorbed into the broth.) DO NOT TOUCH THAT LIQUID. Just bring the heat down and allow it to simmer. If you notice any scum on the surface of the broth, spoon it off.

4. Remove the entire breasts from the chicken, and using two forks, finely shred all that white meat, and return it to the broth. If you'd prefer, you could also cut it into bite-size pieces, and you could choose to cut and add in the dark meat as well. (If not, hit it with a pinch of salt and pop it into your mouth for pure poultry pleasure.)

5. Also back into the simmering broth go that diced parsnip, turnip, and leek, together with some salt and pepper. Let it simmer for about 15 minutes. Adjust seasoning. Serve in bowls, topped with either finely chopped dill fronds or parsley or scallions.

6. Congratulations. You have made world-class chicken soup from scratch. And how good does your home smell?

POTATO LEEK SOUP (*POTAGE PARMENTIER*)

It has often been said that there's nothing like a thick and creamy bowl of hot soup on a cold day, right? Well, this one's plenty thick, but uses no cream whatsoever. Instead, good old potatoes beautifully flavored by leeks provide the smooth and hearty bowl of goodness.

Note: Always be super careful when blending hot liquids, such as soup. The steam heat can literally blow the lid off the top of a blender. So you need to vent. (Who doesn't?) In this case, that means to remove the stopper from the blender top and cover it with a cloth before pulsing. Better yet, think about investing in one of those immersion blenders that goes right into the pot itself.

8 SERVINGS

INGREDIENTS
3 LEEKS, WHITE PART ONLY, WELL CLEANED*, TRIMMED
1½ TEASPOONS OIL
4 CUPS WATER, CHICKEN STOCK, OR A COMBINATION OF BOTH
1½ POUNDS PEELED POTATOES, ROUGHLY CUT INTO CHUNKS (YUKON GOLD POTATOES ARE GOOD, BUT OTHERS WORK)
SALT AND FRESHLY GROUND BLACK PEPPER TO TASTE
CROUTONS OR PARMESAN CHEESE FOR GARNISH (OPTIONAL)

PREPARATION

1. Cut the leek into 1-inch pieces; you should have a good 2–3 cups' worth.

2. Heat the oil in a stockpot, add leeks, and cook ("sweat") over medium heat for 3 or 4 minutes, or until the leeks begins to wilt.

3. Pour in liquid and add the potatoes and give it a good hit of salt. Bring to a boil, then reduce the heat and cover, boiling gently for 30–40 minutes, until vegetables are very tender. Remove any foam or scum that rises to surface with a spoon or ladle.

4. Blend to thick and creamy with either a blender or processor. Taste and adjust seasonings if needed. Serve hot, garnished with croutons or sprinkled with fresh Parmesan cheese. Soup can also be cooled and frozen.

* Cleaning leeks: Cut off the hard, green outer leaves of the leeks (the softer, light green is okay) and trim the root end. Split the leek in half lengthwise and fan open under running water, washing it well inside to remove any and all sand or dirt.

SOUTH OF THE BORDER CORN, TOMATO, AND BLACK BEAN SALAD

Anyone who is fortunate enough to live near a part of the country where tomatoes and corn grow locally looks forward to that point during the summer when the flood of fabulously fresh produce arrives. You don't really need to do much with them when corn and tomatoes are at their peak, but I like to add a third dimension of taste and texture—black beans—and then dress simply with lime juice, olive oil, and a sprinkling of fresh herbs, such as cilantro or oregano. Sweet, juicy, and savory—it's good eating. Especially next to some sizzling steak just off the grill.

INGREDIENTS

4 EARS OF FRESH CORN

3–4 MEDIUM SIZE TOMATOES, CORED AND DICED

8 OUNCES (½ CAN) BLACK BEANS, RINSED

¼ CUP LIME JUICE

¼ CUP OLIVE OIL

½ TEASPOON SALT

3 TEASPOONS CILANTRO (OR LESS THAN THAT FOR OTHER FRESH HERBS, LIKE OREGANO)

PREPARATION

1. Bring large pot of water to a boil, and cook corn for 2–3 minutes.

2. Remove corn from pot and set aside to cool.

3. When cool, slice kernels from cobs with a sharp knife.

4. Combine cut corn, tomatoes, and black beans in a large bowl.

5. Toss together with the rest of the ingredients, and taste for seasoning (but you knew that).

SuperBowls—Noodles, Soups, and Salads

161

FRESH AND EASY WATERMELON, TOMATO, AND FETA SALAD

At first, it seemed like an odd combination. But once I tasted it I was sold. Sweetness from watermelon, coupled with a touch of acidity from the tommies, a hit of creamy saltiness from the cheese, accented by the fragrant basil. All good. And a great way to stimulate the appetite before serving something savory from the grill. (Speaking of which, grilling watermelon slices is a big idea. Try it, it works.)

SERVES 4

INGREDIENTS
1 POUND SEEDLESS WATERMELON, RIND REMOVED
1 POUND RIPE TOMATOES
4 OUNCES FETA CHEESE
2 TABLESPOONS EXTRA VIRGIN OLIVE OIL
ABOUT 8 FRESH BASIL LEAVES
SEA SALT, TO TASTE

PREPARATION

1. Cut watermelon into chunks and slice the tomatoes into wedges, keeping everything approximately the same size.

2. Combine in a bowl.

3. Crumble feta over the mixture, and add olive oil and basil, torn by hand.

4. Season with sea salt and toss gently.

Salads

So often, salads are forgettable. I think that's because they're generally served as the precursor to something else we call the "main course." Their ingredients are uninspiring, their composition haphazard, and their dressing either over- or under-whelming. A shameful waste of perfectly good stomach space.

Then there are the salads that pleasure your taste buds and stimulate your palate. So irresistible that you don't want them to end. That is a sexy salad.

So what does it take to have one?

1. **FRESHNESS.** The components should be fresh, not canned or frozen. There are exceptions (marinated artichoke hearts, water chestnuts, beans), but very few. Straight-from-the-garden matters.

2. **TEXTURE.** You need texture. I like the crispiness of romaine, but whatever lettuce you choose as your base, it should be supplemented by shredded vegetables that have crunch; carrots and purple cabbage are ideal. Croutons are fabulous when they're homemade—if not, you're eating stale bread. Nuts and seeds are a delight.

3. **INGREDIENTS.** Not counting the lettuce, more than six or seven ingredients is generally overkill. Choose veggies (carrots, cukes, mushrooms, tommies), your protein (chicken, tuna, turkey), a corresponding cheese (blue, Parm, feta), and a little extra "something something," like pine nuts. They rock; sunflower seeds are brilliant, too. Craisins don't suck.

4. **CHOP IT.** I'm not sure what we did before they routinely started chopping salad. But I've taken a poll, and people want their salad chopped. Making it at home? You'll want to own a "*double mezzaluna*."

5. **DRESSING.** Do not overdress. Drowning a salad is a cardinal sin. And unless you're going with nothing but a wedge of iceberg and crispy bacon bits—perfect with blue cheese dressing—avoid the creamy kinds that tend to dominate. The dressing is not the star, but a supporting player. A simple vinaigrette allows the salad's constituents to shine.

BIG AND BOLD TOMATO, GORGONZOLA, AND OLIVE SALAD

When tomatoes are in peak season they are pretty good on their own with a soupçon* of coarse salt. But if you want to make an *exciting* and *bold* salad featuring tomatoes, this one displays a whole lot of big, explosive flavors. Pretty impressive to look at and even better to taste.

*I was determined to use the word soupçon somewhere in this book. It's a very small quantity, by the way.

SERVES 8

INGREDIENTS
6 LARGE TOMATOES, SLICED
2 TABLESPOONS VINEGAR
4–5 TABLESPOONS OLIVE OIL
SALT AND PEPPER
⅓ CUP HALVED AND PITTED KALAMATA OLIVES
⅓ CUP CRUMBLED BLUE CHEESE, LIKE GORGONZOLA (ABOUT 2 OUNCES)
2 TABLESPOONS DRAINED CAPERS
FRESH BASIL LEAVES

PREPARATION

1. Arrange tomatoes on large platter.
2. Drizzle with vinegar, then oil.
3. Sprinkle lightly with salt and fresh grated pepper.
4. Top with olives, blue cheese, and capers.
5. Garnish with basil leaves and send Instagram photo to @shortorderdad.

GRAPEFRUIT AVOCADO SALAD

If you can get your hands on juicy, pink grapefruit and perfectly ripe avocados, then consider combining them into this wonderful and good looking salad. Their best individual characteristics—the sweet and tart of grapefruit, the creamy richness of avocado—complement each other rather beautifully. The concept is simple and the dressing can be as well. The execution, however, does require a certain dexterity to cut and slice the elements properly so that you end up with clean grapefruit segments (without pits or the white pith) and slender avocado slices of roughly equal size. If so, you win.

Note: Save whatever grapefruit juice you can as cut them, and add it to whatever dressing you use. You can always use a basic vinaigrette, or just splash a little olive oil and a touch of vinegar across the top.

4 SERVINGS

INGREDIENTS
2 HASS AVOCADOS, PEELED AND SLICED ¼ INCH
   THICK
2 LARGE PINK (OR RUBY RED) GRAPEFRUITS,
   PEELED, SEGMENTED, ANY SEEDS REMOVED
VINAIGRETTE
SALT AND PEPPER TO TASTE

PREPARATION

1. Alternate the avocado slices and grapefruit segments on a platter.

2. Spoon vinaigrette on top, sprinkle with salt and pepper, and serve immediately.

NOT YOUR MOMMA'S TUNA SALAD

(or How to Titillate Your Tuna)

Tuna conjures up a number of images for me. It used to be that smelly stuff that came out of a can, sold as either Solid White or Chunk Light, in water or oil. Tuna has since graduated from those days to include the kind eaten raw at the sushi bar. Particularly sublime is the fatty variety that comes from the belly, the *otoro*. But you can feed a family of four for what a single piece of that costs. There's also the seared tuna one often sees on restaurant menus, nicely charred and peppery on the outside, often served pretty rare on the inside. "Black & blue," the chefs call it. Delightful.

Still the most popular is canned tuna, often blended with mayo and whatever else, generally served in a sandwich or scooped over salad. This is the tuna I recall from childhood. With disgust. It's not that I didn't like "tuna fish salad," as they called it. It's just that by lunchtime in school the sandwich my mother had made for me—with mayo, onion, and celery on white bread—was completely soggy, the tuna was warm, and it smelled, and looked . . . like cat food. All in all, a depressing, soaking wet, stinking mess . . . that I never ate. Thankfully she also put chips and a banana in my Superman lunch box, so at least I had something to munch on.

Well, I have new appreciation for tuna "salad" these days, perhaps nostalgic—but never enough to make it with onion and celery, my recollection still haunted by the mess in my third grade lunch box. Instead I throw in variety of readily available ingredients that bring flavor, texture, and excitement to yesteryear's "tuna salad." As I said, this is not your mother's tuna salad. Although the secret ingredient*, ironically, was suggested to me by . . . my very own mother.

SERVES 1

INGREDIENTS

1 (7-OUNCE) CAN TUNA
1–2 TEASPOONS MAYONNAISE
1 TEASPOON DRAINED CAPERS
* 1 TEASPOON SWEET GREEN PICKLE RELISH
1 TEASPOON PICKLE JUICE (IF YOU HAPPEN TO HAVE IT ON HAND)
SRIRACHA TO TASTE, OPTIONAL

Note: You could also squeeze in a squirt of fresh lemon, chop in some fresh herbs, like dill, and why not even mash up some potato chips and throw those in as well.

PREPARATION

1. In a medium bowl, combine all the ingredients and mix with a fork until thoroughly combined.

2. Serve over lettuce or on your favorite sandwich bread. Make sure to have some potato chips on the side. Just in case.

CHAPTER ELEVEN

A LITTLE SOMETHING ON THE SIDE

SAUTÉED GREENS (KALE, COLLARDS, OR CHARD)

I have no recollection whatsoever of eating fresh greens as a kid. Maybe string beans. But certainly nothing leafy. Even spinach came frozen. Yet if you go to the average grocery store these days you can find a wide array of leafy vegetables that I never even knew existed as a youngster. Kale, Swiss chard, collards, dandelion greens, mustard greens, and so on. Whichever you decide upon, I find that they're at their best when simply prepared with olive oil, garlic, and salt. Maybe a squeeze of lemon.

Note: The directions below call for quickly steaming the greens before sautéing them. However, you can skip that and go directly to the sauté if you want. That works better for softer greens, such as spinach, but less well for those that are firmer, such as kale, which require a bit more cooking to soften.

SERVES 4

INGREDIENTS
2 POUNDS FRESH, LEAFY GREEN VEGETABLES

2 TABLESPOONS EXTRA-VIRGIN OLIVE OIL (THERE'S NOTHING WRONG WITH BUTTER EITHER, IF YOU PREFER)

2 GARLIC CLOVES, THINLY SLICED

SALT AND PEPPER TO TASTE

FRESHLY SQUEEZED LEMON JUICE, TO TASTE (OPTIONAL)

PREPARATION

1. Clean and rinse the veggies well.
2. Don't dry them. Instead, cook them in a covered pan over medium heat with salt and whatever water clings to them from the washing. Three minutes or so is fine, or until they're tender.
3. Drain and dry the pan.
4. Add oil and garlic and cook on medium high for a minute or two until garlic turns just a slight nutty brown.
5. Add the greens and toss around for another couple of minutes.
6. Taste and adjust seasoning.
7. Add a squeeze of lemon, if you like.
8. Serve away.

CHOPPIN' BROCCOLI (WITH GARLIC AND OIL)

Like many others, my kids had no interest in broccoli. Not steamed. Not roasted. No way. No how. Then something happened. I think it was at a pizza place. We ordered the broccoli with garlic and oil. And it came all soft and chopped up. And my kids ate it up. Loved it. So much so that we often start restaurant meals now with chopped broccoli instead of the usual loaf of bread. Who knew?

Note: Save some of the cooking water . . . it might come in handy.

INGREDIENTS

1 BUNCH BROCCOLI, TRIMMED AND CUT INTO PIECES
2–3 TABLESPOONS OLIVE OIL
2–3 CLOVES GARLIC, PEELED AND SLICED THIN
SALT AND PEPPER

PREPARATION

1. In a pot of salted water, boil or steam the broccoli until cooked, either *al dente* or softer.

2. Remove and chop it finely.

3. Heat olive oil in a sauté pan, and toast the garlic until it just starts to turn a little golden.

4. Toss in the broccoli, salt, and pepper, and toss it all around. If you feel like it throw in a spoon of that broccoli cooking water for a makeshift "sauce."

5. Now insist that your kids re-think broccoli. Best of luck with that.

Note: Go right ahead and roast that broccoli if you want. It's superb that way, too.

RIGHTEOUS ROASTED VEGETABLES (CAULIFLOWER, FENNEL, AND/OR BRUSSELS SPROUTS)

Apparently they didn't make these veggies back in the day because I don't remember eating these, either. But I do recall those that came out of a can (carrots and peas seemed to be popular, and horrid) and others that were of the frozen variety (like peas, not terrible). I certainly didn't eat cauliflower, fennel, or Brussels sprouts. That has definitely changed, due primarily to the revelation I had when learning about roasting them. Wow, what a difference! When caramelization kicks in, these vegetables get transformed into something delectable. And all you really need is some olive oil and salt. The basic recipe and process can be used for any root vegetable, which can be made individually, or combined with others.

Notes:
1) This is an "either/or" recipe, which is to say that you could make any of these individually or combine them. If combining you'll want to cut all the veggies to approximately the same size so that they'll be finished cooking at the same time.
2) Cauliflower can also be cut into thick slices they call "steaks" and roasted the same way. Or, and I've done this too (as you can see in the picture on page 168), you can oil, salt, and roast the entire head of cauliflower. It makes for a dramatic presentation.

ANY OF THESE THREE VEGETABLES WOULD SERVE 4

INGREDIENTS
1 HEAD CAULIFLOWER, CHOPPED INTO FLORETS
OR . . .
2 BULBS OF FENNEL, SLICED,
OR . . .
2 CUPS OF BRUSSELS SPROUTS, TRIMMED AND CUT
   IN HALF LENGTHWISE
ENOUGH OLIVE OIL TO COAT THE VEGGIES (AROUND
   2 TABLESPOONS, MORE IF NECESSARY)
SALT AND PEPPER TO TASTE

PREPARATION

1. Preheat oven to 425°F.
2. Toss vegetables in a bowl with olive oil to coat, then season well with salt and pepper.
3. Place vegetables in a single layer on a baking sheet and cook until they get fragrant and nicely browned. You might flip them once along the way to ensure that both sides caramelize. You want them to be crisp and brown on the outside and tender within. That could take anywhere between 15–30 minutes, depending on how much color you want. I think you want more.

You can serve them just as they are, and they're not bad cold, either. They can also be dressed up with a splash of vinegar, a toss of crispy bacon bits, or a handful of toasted pine nuts, for example. Or serve with one of my many sauces—like red pepper, *chimichurri*, pesto, or *gremolata*—to elevate this dish even further.

WHO YOU CALLIN' GARBANZO, CHICKPEA? (ROASTED CHICKPEAS WITH *PIMENTÓN*) (INTUITIVE)

I dig me some chickpeas, also known as garbanzos, the little legumes packed with protein. Plenty of people pop 'em in salad, as they are, generally out of a can. Eh. For me, the real treat occurs when you roast (or toast) them. The heat not only develops their buttery, nutlike flavor, it gives them a slightly crunchy exterior that, combined with a tender, mellow interior, is an altogether winning combination. Easy-peasy to do, plus you can personalize them in innumerable ways, depending entirely on your own taste preferences. Ready?

INGREDIENTS
12-OUNCE CAN OF CHICKPEAS, DRAINED AND RINSED
1 TABLESPOON OLIVE OIL
½ TEASPOON KOSHER SALT
1 TEASPOON SMOKED PAPRIKA (*PIMENTÓN*) OR DRIED SPICE SEASONING OF YOUR CHOOSING (SUCH AS CHILI POWDER, CUMIN, GARAM MASALA, ETC.)

PREPARATION

1. Preheat oven to 400°F.

2. Drain and rinse a 12-ounce can of chickpeas and toss them with the olive oil until coated.

3. Season with salt, plus the other flavors you enjoy (e.g., chili powder, cayenne pepper, cumin, garlic powder, etc.).

4. Mix around to distribute the spice coating and spread them out on a baking sheet and roast until browned and a little crunchy on the outside, but still a tad mushy inside. Depending on your oven, that should be about 15 minutes, but keep an eye on them so as not to burn.

5. Enjoy them straight up, as a snack, or pop them into your salad.

Note: You can also make these right in the toaster oven.

- -

ROAST YOUR ASPARAGUS

Nothing quite says springtime eating like asparagus. Sure, you can get it year round, but the tastiest asparagus appears when the worst of winter is over and temperatures start to rise. Your best option is to try to locate some at a farmer's market, but if you don't have one nearby, be sure to ask the produce people in your supermarket when the asparagus arrived in the store and from where it came. Closer and fresher is what you're looking for.

I generally roast asparagus these days because the caramelization they achieve from the oven makes them thoroughly delectable. And it's quite easy too: Trim off the hard bottom part of the stem, which you can do by hand because they snap right where they're supposed to. Then just give 'em a quick rinse, lay them in a single layer on a baking sheet, douse with olive oil, sprinkle on salt, and bake at 425°F until they get good and brown. Generally about 15–20 minutes.

Note: Grated lemon zest on this before or after roasting is a win.

BRILLIANT BRAISED LEEKS (*POIREAUX ETUVÉS*)

One of my favorite discoveries from French cooking school days was braised leeks, simply seasoned with salt, pepper, and olive oil or butter. Popular in French cuisine, the leek—along with onions, shallots, and garlic—is a member of the Alliaceae family. Now it's also a member of my family. Though pungent, when slow-cooked and simmered, leeks become silky and sumptuous while developing a delicate sweet flavor. This classic recipe is easy to make, especially after you get past the rather tedious task of cleaning these dirt-laden vegetables. You'll quickly realize that the fuss was well worth the effort when you take your first bite, however. A great way to impress your guests is to present the dish by its French name, *poireaux étuvés*. Serve them as a vegetable side dish to any roasted meat or seafood entrée. Or serve cold as an appetizer with my classic vinaigrette (page 194). Bon appétit!

SERVES 4 TO 6

INGREDIENTS
6 LARGE LEEKS
FILTERED WATER (COULD SUBSTITUTE OR SUPPLEMENT WITH DRY WHITE WINE OR CHICKEN STOCK)
KOSHER SALT AND FRESHLY CRACKED BLACK PEPPER
2 TABLESPOONS EXTRA VIRGIN OLIVE OIL OR UNSALTED BUTTER

PREPARATION

1. To clean leeks, remove any bruised leaves and trim the root ends, keeping the leaves attached. Discard the very fibrous upper dark green part, and halve the white to light green parts lengthwise. Completely rinse the leaves under cold running water, "fanning" the leaves to remove all dirt. Drain.

2. In a large sauté pan place leeks cut side down in a single layer. Add the liquid to about halfway up the side of the leeks. Season with salt and pepper to taste and add the oil or butter. Cover and simmer over low heat until the liquid has almost fully evaporated and the leeks are tender, 20–25 minutes. (If necessary, add a couple of tablespoons of water at a time along the way to prevent the leeks from browning. Conversely, if the leeks are tender you can remove the cover to facilitate evaporation.) Do I really need to tell you what to do with them when they're ready?

GLAZED CARROTS

Although you could roast carrots like other root vegetables (see recipe, page 175), when you braise them simply with nothing more than water, oil or butter, and salt, they get soft, delectable, and naturally sweet. If you want to pump up the sweetness factor a bit, you can simply sprinkle on a touch of sugar. In that case, I suppose you could call them *candied* carrots instead, a name change that I've learned is even more attractive to kids than glazed. Unless, of course, you're referring to doughnuts.

Note: Glazing is a good way to prepare any number of root vegetables, such as parsnips, turnips, celery root, and even baby onions.

SERVES 4

INGREDIENTS
1 BUNCH CARROTS, PEELED
WATER
1 TABLESPOON BUTTER OR OLIVE OIL
SALT AND PEPPER TO TASTE
1 TEASPOON SUGAR (OPTIONAL)

PREPARATION

1. Place the carrots in a pan large enough to hold them in a single layer.

2. Add enough water to come halfway up the carrots.

3. Add fat of your choice, salt and pepper, and sugar, if using.

4. Bring to boil, then to low simmer, and cook until carrots are tender and the liquid has evaporated. To give the carrots a darker glaze, add a touch of water and roll the carrots around as you "deglaze" the pan.

5. Serve hot.

SPICY GREEN BEANS GANGNAM STYLE

You might not have heard of *gochujang* yet, but it is becoming increasingly popular. If you like it a little spicy, this Korean hot chile paste is marvelous. I use it as the base of a pungent dressing for green beans, but it would work for many other veggies. Unlike your basic hot sauce, I find that there's something about *gochujang* that is appealing even to those who normally shy away from the hot stuff. By balancing out the dressing with the addition of acidity to brighten it up and sweetness to work against the spice, you create a sweet heat that is pretty irresistible. Cilantro adds a dash of freshness and fragrance. Plus, when you top those green beans with crunchy bacon bits and a handful of nuts, you've got yourself a winner.

SERVES 4

INGREDIENTS
1 POUND GREEN BEANS
1 TABLESPOON OIL
4–5 STRIPS OF BACON, COOKED CRISP AND
    CRUMBLED (RESERVE 1–2 TEASPOONS OF BACON
    FAT)
2 TABLESPOONS *GOCHUJANG* PASTE
1 TABLESPOON (OR MORE) RICE WINE VINEGAR (YES,
    OTHERS OKAY IF YOU DON'T HAVE THE RICE WINE)
2 TEASPOONS HONEY
SMALL HANDFUL FINELY CHOPPED CILANTRO
    (OPTIONAL, BUT LOVELY IF YOU HAVE)
1 GENEROUS HANDFUL PINE (OR OTHER) NUTS
    (ABOUT 3–4 TABLESPOONS)

PREPARATION

1. Preheat oven to 425°F.

2. Blanch (page 44) the string beans in boiling water for a couple of minutes to minimize their stiffness just a little. (They'll also turn a vibrant green color.) You could skip this step and proceed directly to roasting them, but I find that this quick blanch helps to maintain a nice chew to the bean after roasting, rather than total crispness. (Come to think of it, you could also blanch or steam the beans until ready and skip the roasting step altogether.) When roasting, toss beans first with oil.

3. While they're cooking, *crispy* up some bacon. (I realize that crispy isn't a verb, but it should be.)

4. Crumble it into chunky pieces, set it aside, and reserve the bacon fat.

5. To make the dressing, whisk together the *gochujang*, vinegar, and honey with a teaspoon or so of the bacon fat until well blended. (Because the *gochujang* is very thick, you can add more vinegar or oil or even a splash of water if necessary to thin it.) Mix in the cilantro if using.

6. Top the string beans with the bacon and nuts, pour in a little dressing at a time (to taste), and toss the whole shebang together. Crazy good, am I right? Then take a bow, receive applause.

BAKED POTATO "FRIES"

I'm pretty sure that French fries would win the popularity contest for all-time favorite food in the world. I don't even own a deep fryer, although you could put a lot of oil in any old deep pot and fry away. Instead, I cut potatoes into whatever shape feels right that day, coat them in olive oil, and toss 'em into the oven to cook until crispy and golden brown. They're easier to make and much less fatty than the original way. And they're good. Very good. I haven't had anyone complain yet. Plus, you can flavor them with your favorite dried herbs and spices, like rosemary, oregano, or chili powder.

SERVES 6

INGREDIENTS
2½ POUNDS (ABOUT 6 MEDIUM) WAXY UNPEELED
    POTATOES, CUT INTO 1-INCH CUBES
½ CUP OLIVE OIL
SALT

PREPARATION

1. Pre-heat oven to 425°F.

2. In large roasting pan or baking sheet, combine potatoes and oil.

3. Stir until potatoes are well coated, and spread them evenly in pan.

4. Roast in oven until golden brown and crispy, around 35–45 minutes.

5. Remove and transfer to serving dish.

6. Sprinkle with salt to taste, and serve immediately.

POTATOES RÖSTI

Some people might recognize this as the national dish of Switzerland. To me, it's the world's largest potato pancake. What makes it awesome is a totally crispy outside, covering a soft, creamy potato inside. Here's another thing to love about this: No egg, no flour, no nothing. Just potatoes. Not that there's nothing at all wrong with adding a little onion (or leek) if you have it around.

I don't make these in the usual way, which would have you cook the potatoes first prior to frying. One step too many for me. Instead, I grate and proceed directly to frying. You have an option as to the type of fat you can use. Nothing at all wrong with oil or butter, or both, for that matter. But if you happen to get your hands on some duck fat (because you've made my seared duck breasts, page 106, and reserved the fat), go for the glory! Whichever fat you choose, the hotter it is before introducing the potatoes the better, for they will absorb less fat. But you'll need to be very careful when plopping the potatoes in because they will splatter. Splattering hot oil is no fun for the entire family.

Oh, another thing: These can be made entirely on top of the stove *or* finished in the oven, in which case you'd need a pan that can be used for both. And it needs to be wide enough to hold a whole load of grated potatoes. Plus, and this is key, those potatoes need to be very—and I mean Sahara—well-drained and dried. Use a salad spinner, use paper towels, use a kitchen towel—or all three—whatever it takes to squeeze all of the excess moisture from the potatoes before cooking.

SERVES 4

INGREDIENTS
4 POTATOES
2 TEASPOONS SALT (OR TO TASTE) AND FRESHLY
    GROUND PEPPER (ALSO TO TASTE)
OPTIONAL: ¼ CUP GRATED ONION OR LEEK
3 TABLESPOONS OIL OR BUTTER OR DUCK FAT FOR
    FRYING; *MORE AS NEEDED*

PREPARATION

1. Peel the potatoes and grate them coarsely by hand, if you can bear to, or by the grating blade on the food processor, if you have one of those.

2. Squeeze as much liquid as possible out of them. A salad spinner is a start, plus you'll need to squeeze a handful at a time—in paper or kitchen towel—and transfer to a dry bowl. Do not worry if the potatoes begin to discolor a bit, just make sure they're well drained. Mix in salt, pepper, and grated onion or leek, if using, to combine.

3. Heat half the fat in a heavy-based frying pan over medium high heat until very hot. Carefully (as the oil will spatter) add a ladleful of potato at a time until all the potatoes are crowded in. Then press down by spatula or with a fork, molding and forming it into a flat cake that fits snugly into the skillet.

4. Adjust the heat so that it sizzles, but you *do not* want the bottom browning too rapidly. Shake the skillet

occasionally—you want the potatoes to stick to each other, not to the pan—and cook until the underside turns a deep golden brown, around 10–15 minutes. Using a spatula, carefully lift and check underneath to see that they're good and crisp. At that point, slide a knife around the perimeter so that the potatoes are not stuck to the side of the pan.

5. Now comes the fun part. Don't flip out, flip the potatoes. Position a plate facedown right on top of the potatoes. Holding it against the potatoes, invert the pan so that the potatoes slide out and you end up with the pancake sitting cooked side up on the plate. Got it? Good. Now spread the remaining fat around the pan and as soon as it's hot, slide the potato cake back into it so that the crisp side is face up and the undercooked side is against the pan bottom. Well done. (You! Not the potatoes.)

6. Cook for another 10 minutes or so until the new bottom is also well browned and crispy. (The option here is that you could finish the cooking in the oven instead, in which case it should be preheated to 425°F, and the cooking time to complete will be about 10–15 minutes, depending on thickness.)

7. If you have the nerve, carefully remove the whole pancake from the pan to present it on a platter. Alternatively, you could leave it in the (very hot) pan and slice or scoop into wedges directly from there. Maybe toss a little green herb on top, like chopped parsley or a spring of rosemary. (See, now you're "plating.") However you do it, you're a hero. Perhaps even more so if you accompany it with my grandmother's applesauce (page 207) or a dollop of crème fraîche or sour cream. I won't even mention caviar. Or vodka.

OVEN ROASTED CHERRY TOMATOES (ARE YOUR FRIEND)

Cherry tomatoes are available pretty much all year-round. When they're good, they're a fine addition to salads. I like to roast them, however, which renders them softer and sweeter. The longer you roast them, the more concentrated their flavor becomes. They're nifty on top of a burger or as a simple topping to many main courses. Or you could also turn them into a quick tomato sauce easily by adding oil and/or stock and blending them after roasting.

INGREDIENTS

3 CUPS SMALL TOMATOES (CHERRY, GRAPE, PLUM),
   SLICED IN HALF LENGTHWISE

2 TABLESPOONS OLIVE OIL

SALT AND PEPPER TO TASTE

2 GARLIC CLOVES, PEELED AND SLICED INTO
   QUARTERS (OPTIONAL)

PREPARATION

1. Preheat oven to 350°F.

2. Mix tomatoes, oil, salt and pepper, and garlic, if using.

3. Roast on baking sheet for about 30 minutes, or until tomatoes have softened and shriveled a bit, and there's no liquid remaining in the roasting pan.

GRILLED CORN MEXICAN-STYLE

Commonly sold from street carts, this combination of Mexican flavors makes corn tongue-tingling. The usual recipe slathers on mayonnaise, but mine does not because my people don't like it all . . . "gooey," I think is the correct food term. The key here is to get some char on the corn, which can be accomplished on the grill or in a grill pan. I like it with crumbly Mexican cheese, but you can also substitute other grated cheeses (like Parmesan) for a similar effect. Viva Mexico!

SERVES 4

INGREDIENTS
4 EARS CORN, HUSKED

1 LIME, JUICED (ABOUT 2 TABLESPOONS), PLUS 1 LIME CUT INTO 4 WEDGES, FOR SERVING

¼ TEASPOON CHILI (OR ANCHO CHILE) POWDER

⅓ CUP CHEESE, CRUMBLED (PREFERABLY MEXICAN, SUCH AS *QUESO FRESCO* OR *COTIJA* CHEESE)

SALT AND FRESHLY GROUND BLACK PEPPER TO TASTE

CAYENNE PEPPER OR HOT SAUCE (OPTIONAL) TO TASTE

4 TABLESPOONS MINCED FRESH CILANTRO

PREPARATION

1. Grill corn until well charred and cooked through, about 10 minutes, more or less.

2. Meanwhile, in a bowl, whisk together lime juice, chili powder, cheese, salt, pepper, and cayenne, if using.

3. Brush this mixture all over cooked corn and top with chopped cilantro.

4. Serve with lime wedges for those wanting an extra blast.

Note: There's another way to play this that's equally as enticing. After grilling the corn, slather it with a Mexican butter "composed" of lime and jalapeño for a kick (recipe page 209).

PINK PEPPERCORN BISCUITS

I love these little treats because they're flaky, fabulous, and fuss-free. Like a few of my friends. (Too few.) Plus those "peppercorn" pieces look cool and have only the slightest bit of peppery bite. (They're not actually peppers.) It's a super simple dough that you form by hand, cut into little squares, and bake until puffy and lightly brown. Go ahead, show everyone you can bake biscuits like grandma. Just don't wear her apron.

MAKES A BUNCH, ABOUT 15

INGREDIENTS
2 CUPS CAKE FLOUR
1 TABLESPOON BAKING POWDER
1 TEASPOON SALT
1 TABLESPOON PINK PEPPERCORNS, LIGHTLY
    CRUSHED
1 CUP CREAM
⅓ CUP MELTED BUTTER

PREPARATION

1. Preheat oven to 425°F.

2. Sift the dry ingredients into a bowl, add peppercorns, and mix all together well.

3. Incorporate cream slowly, stirring to make the dough. You might not need all the cream, but enough for it to form into a ball. Knead the dough for a minute.

4. With a little dough at a time, pat into ½-inch thick squares. If you want neat, cut 'em with a knife.

5. Dip into melted butter, place them an inch or so apart on a baking sheet, and cook for about 12 minutes, until golden in color. Serve warm.

CHAPTER TWELVE

GO-TO SAUCES AND DRESSINGS

CLASSIC VINAIGRETTE

I haven't bought salad dressing in a bottle for as long as I can remember. And that's a very long time. You'll understand why there's no reason to purchase bottled once you make your own. It's as easy as combining oil with either vinegar or lemon and adding a touch of seasoning. There are a lot of variations possible, including the type of acid you use (vinegar, or lemon juice instead) to the type of oil (olive, canola, safflower, etc.), the choice of "aromatic" (shallot or garlic), and any additions you desire, like herbs or grated cheese or curry powder, for example. The proportion of oil to "acid" can also vary; some recipes call for as much as four times as much oil as vinegar—three-to-one is the standard, but others call for two-to-one. The point is that whatever ratio you use and whichever combination of flavorings you settle upon, you get to control the final product to your liking. Not only will you appreciate what you've made more than what you can find on a supermarket shelf, you'll find this sprightly vinaigrette to be very versatile. Good not only on salads, but on grilled meat, fish, or vegetables.

Variations aplenty: Once you master the basic technique, you can start to have some fun with any one of a number of different fats and/or vinegars. Balsamic, of course, but also try sherry wine vinegar or champagne wine vinegar. Among fats, walnut oil is one of the tastes to try as well. (I even deploy duck fat for the vinaigrette on page 106.) Experiment with different chopped herbs in your dressing, especially fresh ones like tarragon or basil.

MAKES 1 CUP

INGREDIENTS
1 TABLESPOON DIJON-STYLE MUSTARD
2 OUNCES WINE VINEGAR (OR FRESHLY SQUEEZED LEMON JUICE)
1 SMALL SHALLOT, FINELY MINCED (OR 1 CLOVE OF GARLIC)
¼ TEASPOON SALT, OR TO TASTE
FRESH GROUND PEPPER TO TASTE
6 OUNCES OIL (TRY OLIVE, PEANUT, CANOLA, OR SAFFLOWER)

PREPARATION

Combine mustard, vinegar, shallot, salt, and grind in fresh pepper. Slowly whisk in oil until all is blended and smooth.

BEURRE BLANC (WHITE BUTTER SAUCE)

Beurre blanc is one of those classic sauces you learn to make in French cooking school. It is a white butter sauce with acidity that plays perfectly against a piece of fish or with seafood. The key here is *emulsification*, which simply means that you need to whisk constantly and not let the mixture come to a boil until you produce one harmonious, blended sauce.

MAKES 1 CUP

INGREDIENTS

1½ OUNCES OF SHALLOTS, PEELED AND FINELY
   MINCED (2 MEDIUM)
¼ CUP WHITE WINE
¼ CUP WHITE WINE VINEGAR
2 TABLESPOONS WATER (HEAVY CREAM CAN BE
   SUBSTITUTED)
½ POUND UNSALTED BUTTER, CUT INTO LITTLE
   (1-INCH) CUBES
SALT AND PEPPER TO TASTE

PREPARATION

1. Combine the shallots with the white wine and vinegar in a saucepan and gently simmer until *almost* all of the liquid has evaporated. Add in the water, and if there's any browning inside the saucepan wipe it away with a wet paper towel. (You don't want it to discolor the final sauce.)

2. Over medium high heat add butter to the shallot mixture a little at a time, whisking constantly, until all the butter is incorporated into the mixture, and the texture is creamy. (Reminder: don't let it boil.)

3. Add salt and pepper, then taste for seasoning. You can add a touch of vinegar if you think the sauce needs to be a bit brighter, or more butter if it seems too acidic. You can strain the sauce or not, depending on whether or not you want the shallots in the sauce. Use immediately over simply prepared fish.

BEURRE NOISETTE (BROWN BUTTER SAUCE)

This is some easy-peasy. Seriously, forget the recipe. Get a stick of butter—or half a stick—and start melting it slowly over medium heat, maybe a touch higher. Now keep going. As the water content evaporates, you'll notice white solids coagulating on the surface. Turn the heat down and when that white stuff turns a pale brown, take the pan off the heat. Your butter has turned a bit brown, right? Good, you want that. And it smells pretty good, too? Kinda nutty. The smell, I'm talking about. Cool. I mean literally, let it cool down to warm before you hit it with a squeeze of lemon juice. (Half a lemon's worth for half a bar of butter; the whole lemon juiced for a whole 8-ounce bar of butter.) Congrats. You've just made your first beurre noisette ("hazelnut butter").

How to use it? Over simply prepared fish, or poached chicken, with vegetables, omelets, or pasta.

PROPER PESTO

With only five key ingredients and just five minutes to make in a blender, pesto is the intensely fragrant and full-flavored basil-based sauce that's perfect for pasta. It's versatile too, as good on a sandwich, a pizza, in soup, or as a dip.

MAKES ABOUT 2 CUPS

INGREDIENTS

2 CUPS FRESH BASIL LEAVES (STEMS REMOVED)

2 TABLESPOONS PINE NUTS (WALNUTS, HAZELNUTS, OR OTHERS CAN BE SUBSTITUTED)

1–2 LARGE CLOVES GARLIC

½ CUP EXTRA-VIRGIN OLIVE OIL

½ CUP FRESHLY GRATED PARMESAN CHEESE

PREPARATION

1. Combine basil leaves, pine nuts, and garlic in a food processor and process until very finely minced.

2. With the blender running, stream in the olive oil until the mixture is smooth.

3. Add the cheese and pulse briefly to combine.

4. Parmesan is salty, but as always, taste to decide if it needs any salt and/or pepper.

ROASTED RED PEPPER PUREE

The truth is I don't love red pepper. I don't hate it either. But this puree is a breeze to make, wonderful to look at, and serves a number of valuable purposes. You can use it as a sauce by spooning it over a cooked piece of fish or meat. You can cultivate your own culinary artistry by laying a pool of it down on a plate and placing foods atop it. You could ladle a dollop on a bowl of hearty soup. Or just serve it as is—as a dip—with some pita chips on the side. Fresh herbs (oregano, marjoram) can be a delightful addition; or use some of the puree in your next vinaigrette. In the age of multitasking, roasted red pepper puree definitely fits the bill.

FYI: You could call it by its French name, *coulis* (coo' lee).

MAKES ABOUT 1 CUP

INGREDIENTS

1 CUP ROASTED RED PEPPERS FROM A JAR,
  DRAINED
1½ TABLESPOON EXTRA-VIRGIN OLIVE OIL
2 GARLIC CLOVES, PEELED
¼ TEASPOON DRIED CRUSHED RED PEPPER
SALT AND PEPPER

PREPARATION

1. Puree all ingredients in processor until smooth.

2. Season with salt and pepper.

Can be made ahead and chilled for a day, covered. Best at room temperature before using.

CHIMICHURRI

Chimichurri is the vibrant green sauce that Argentines typically serve with their famed grilled steaks. The predominant tastes come from parsley, oregano, and vinegar, which is intensified by the addition of garlic and red pepper flakes. Easily made if you have a blender, and your friends and family will be impressed with your sauce-making skills.

To the basic ingredients listed below you can feel free to add a little fresh cilantro (¼ cup), a jalapeño if you like it more spicy, and fresh lime juice if you want to brighten it up. If the sauce seems too thick, you can always thin it down with a bit more vinegar or even a few shots of good old water.

MAKES ABOUT 1 CUP OF SAUCE

INGREDIENTS

1 CUP PACKED FLAT LEAF PARSLEY

2 CLOVES GARLIC, PEELED

⅓ CUP RED WINE VINEGAR

1 TABLESPOON FRESH LIME JUICE

½ CUP OLIVE OIL

1 TABLESPOON DICED (RED) ONION

2 TABLESPOONS FRESH OREGANO (YOU CAN SUBSTITUTE WITH 2 TEASPOONS DRIED OREGANO)

½ TEASPOON CRUSHED RED PEPPER FLAKES

½–1 TEASPOON SALT, OR TO TASTE

PREPARATION

Blend everything in a blender or processor until smooth.

It's fine fresh, but even better if you make it beforehand and refrigerate for a while, even overnight.

THREE SALSAS

TOMATILLO SALSA (SALSA VERDE)

Have you ever enjoyed that green salsa that's often served in Mexican restaurants? Well, it's probably made with tomatillos. Sometimes called Mexican green tomatoes (although they're not actually), tomatillos come with a papery covering that is removed before cooking. The beauty of them is their natural acidity, which is ideal in a salsa, straight up with chips, or as topping for most kinds of grilled meats or chicken. Although the basic ingredients are the same, there are multiple ways to make it. You can chop the ingredients by hand to yield a chunky salsa; you can toss everything into a blender for a smooth salsa (I do); or you can even stew all the ingredients before blending to end up with a smoother, richer sauce.

MAKES ABOUT 2 CUPS

INGREDIENTS

1 POUND FRESH TOMATILLOS, SKINS REMOVED

½ MEDIUM ONION, COARSELY CHOPPED

2 GARLIC CLOVES, PEELED AND CHOPPED

3 TABLESPOONS OLIVE OIL

2–3 TABLESPOONS FRESH SQUEEZED LIME JUICE (TO TASTE)

1–2 SMALL JALAPEÑO (OR SERRANO) PEPPERS, SEEDED AND CHOPPED, DEPENDING ON DESIRED SPICINESS

¼ CUP FRESH CHOPPED CILANTRO

2 TEASPOONS SALT

WATER, IF NECESSARY, TO THIN THE SAUCE

PREPARATION

1. Remove the papery covering from the outside and rinse the tomatillos.

2. Puree tomatillos, onion, garlic, oil, and lime juice in blender, then add peppers, cilantro, and salt, blending until smooth.

3. Let it stand at room temperature for about an hour, then taste for seasoning and adjust accordingly, adding salt, lime juice, or water as necessary.

MANGO TOMATO SALSA

You get sweetness from the mango, acidity from tomato and lime juice, a little bite from onion, heat from jalapeño, and that added fragrant dimension from the cilantro. This stuff is so good people will want to eat it by the spoonful. No need to add oil, though you could. In fact, I take oil out of the equation altogether by throwing corn tortillas right into the oven or toaster oven until they're nice and crisp. Then we all chip and dip away, without the deep-fried packaged chips.

Note: This is a perfect recipe to hone your knife skills, so you may want to hone your knife, too. Sharp knives make a big difference. (And remember: don't put good ones in the dishwasher.)

MAKES 3 CUPS

INGREDIENTS

2 CUPS FRESH, RIPE MANGO, CHOPPED INTO SMALL DICE (2 MANGOES SHOULD WORK)

1 CUP RIPE TOMATO, CHOPPED INTO SMALL DICE (1 LARGE TOMATO SHOULD DO IT)

¼ CUP FINELY CHOPPED ONION

1 GARLIC CLOVE, FINELY MINCED

1 JALAPEÑO OR SERRANO PEPPER, WHITE PITH AND SEEDS REMOVED, VERY FINELY DICED

1 LIME, JUICED (ABOUT 2 TEASPOONS)

½ TEASPOON SALT, OR TO TASTE

3 TABLESPOONS CILANTRO, ROUGHLY CHOPPED

PREPARATION

1. Mix all ingredients together in a bowl.

2. Taste for seasoning, adjusting for salt and lime. Refrigerate and let it sit for at least an hour, or overnight. As good or better the next day after the flavors have had a chance to meld.

TOMATO SALSA

For straight-up tomato salsa, or what they call *salsa cruda*, simply eliminate the mango in the preceding recipe and double up on the tomato instead. Adjust for seasoning, of course.

CRANBERRY SAUCE FOUR WAYS

I understand the excitement over the turkey, the stuffing, and whatever else floats your epicurean boat at the big affair. Me, I like a good cranberry sauce. Its sweet tartness is the perfect foil to offset all that other richness. But never out of a can. Sorry, that won't play. It's far too easy to make it yourself. Here's the basic way and three alternate versions, all of which are of the chunky variety.

#1. Basic version

Makes 2¼ cups. Use fresh berries. If you have frozen, don't defrost them; just add about 2 minutes to the simmering time.

INGREDIENTS

¾ CUP WATER

1 CUP GRANULATED SUGAR

¼ TEASPOON SALT

1 (12-OUNCE) BAG CRANBERRIES (RINSE, AND TOSS ANYTHING THAT AIN'T A CRANBERRY)

PREPARATION

1. Bring water, sugar, and salt to boil in medium saucepan over high heat, stirring occasionally to dissolve sugar.

2. Drop in the crannies and return to a boil, then reduce heat to medium and simmer until slightly thickened. You'll see that most of the berries have popped open after about 7–8 minutes.

3. Transfer to a stainless steel or glass bowl and cool. You can cover and refrigerate for up to 7 days.

#2. Basic plus frozen blueberries added

For a unique and tasty addition, toss in 1 cup of frozen blueberries after the cranberries have already completed popping for a couple of minutes and cook for another five until everything is hot and bubbly.

#3. Cranberry sauce with pears

INGREDIENTS

¾ CUP WATER

1 CUP GRANULATED SUGAR

1 TABLESPOON GRATED FRESH GINGER
¼ TEASPOON GROUND CINNAMON
¼ TEASPOON SALT
1 (12-OUNCE) BAG CRANBERRIES, RINSED AND PICKED THROUGH
2 MEDIUM FIRM, RIPE PEARS, PEELED, CORED, AND CUT INTO ½-INCH CHUNKS

PREPARATION

Bring first five ingredients to boil. Stir in cranberries and pears and return to boil. Then simmer, and follow same process as above.

#4. Go orange!

INGREDIENTS
¾ CUP WATER
1 CUP GRANULATED SUGAR
1 TABLESPOON GRATED ORANGE ZEST
¼ TEASPOON TABLE SALT
1 (12-OUNCE) BAG CRANBERRIES, RINSED AND PICKED THROUGH
2 TABLESPOONS ORANGE LIQUEUR (TRIPLE SEC OR GRAND MARNIER)

PREPARATION

Same as above EXCEPT that you add 1 tablespoon of orange zest to the water, sugar, and salt AND you will add 2 tablespoons of orange liqueur AFTER you take the berries off the heat.

Have fun with it. I've used cinnamon, dry mustard, and ginger, as well as various nuts and dried fruits to add interesting tastes and textures. Or try ruby port instead of the orange liqueur.

And know that cranberries are pretty darn good for you, loaded with antioxidants and vitamins.

MAMA SHERLYE'S APPLESAUCE

It's another one of those few-ingredient recipes you can make with ease rather than buy it out of a jar. Yes, it's better than the bottled kind because it's fresher and can be suited to your taste, but there is also the added satisfaction of having produced it yourself. So there's that, as they say.

MAKES ABOUT 2 CUPS

INGREDIENTS

4 APPLES, PEELED, CORED, AND CHOPPED (CAN BE ASSORTED)
½ CUP WATER
½ TEASPOON GROUND CINNAMON
WHITE SUGAR OR HONEY, TO TASTE (OPTIONAL)

PREPARATION

1. In a saucepan, combine apples, water, and cinnamon. Bring to boil, then reduce to medium heat, cover and cook for 15–20 minutes, until apples are tender and cooked through. (You shouldn't need it, but add a little more water along the way if the apples start to stick to the bottom of the pot.)

2. Mash with a fork or potato masher, to whatever texture you prefer, chunky or smooth. Taste, and season with sugar if so desired. It's good hot or cold.

GREMOLATA

Another fancy name, another really good accompaniment to know about. *Gremolata* is a condiment typically served alongside rich foods such as osso buco, because it deftly counterbalances the inherent richness of a dish by throwing a full-flavor citric blast at it. It brings what they call "brightness." You could also toss it atop roasted vegetables, for example. And you can also replace the lemon zest with orange zest for a change.

INGREDIENTS

½ CUP FLAT LEAF PARSLEY, STEMS REMOVED AND
    FINELY CHOPPED
1 TABLESPOON GRATED LEMON ZEST (MIGHT NEED
    1–2 LEMONS)
1–2 MEDIUM GARLIC CLOVES, FINELY MINCED
    (ABOUT 2 TEASPOONS)

PREPARATION

Mix the ingredients together in a bowl. (Doesn't require salt or olive oil, but feel free.)

JALAPEÑO LIME CILANTRO BUTTER

With flavors from the Mexican profile, this spicy butter brings big taste goodness to almost anything you can imagine—like corn, shrimp, or chicken.

INGREDIENTS

½ POUND UNSALTED BUTTER, SOFTENED

1 TABLESPOON MINCED GARLIC

2 LIMES, JUICED

2 TABLESPOONS CHOPPED CILANTRO

1–2 TABLESPOONS JALAPEÑO, FINELY MINCED, DEPENDING ON YOUR NEED FOR HEAT

SALT AND PEPPER TO TASTE

PREPARATION

1. Combine all the ingredients in a mixing bowl.

2. Season with salt and pepper.

3. Mix well and set aside or refrigerate until ready to use.

CHAPTER THIRTEEN
THE SWEET STUFF

PURE POACHED PEAR PLEASURE

I'm eternally grateful to whoever figured out how to turn grapes into wine. It is also amazing to witness the transformation that takes place when you add sugar to it and heat it up. Eventually, you get syrup. But not just any syrup—it's this intense, gooey, sophisticated, deep rush of *grapiness*. Now, imagine you could enhance that lusciousness even further by adding another flavor dimension to it, and then pour that velvety syrup over softly stewed fruit. Yeah, then make this keeper part of your repertoire and impress your people with your mad skills, rock star.

Note: That flavor enhancement I refer to above is from liqueur and from spice. The liqueur is optional, but good if you have; and you have a choice on the spice mix*, in which either combo below works well.

SERVES 4

INGREDIENTS
1 BOTTLE RED WINE
1 CUP SUGAR
*SPICE MIX: 1 CINNAMON STICK AND 1 TEASPOON VANILLA EXTRACT OR 1 STAR ANISE AND 2 CLOVES
OPTIONAL: 2 SHOTS ORANGE LIQUEUR (SUCH AS COINTREAU, GRAND MARNIER, OR TRIPLE SEC; COULD ALSO USE CRÈME DE CASSIS, MADE OF BLACK CURRANTS)
4 FIRM, RIPE PEARS, PEELED, HALVED LENGTHWISE, CORE/PITS REMOVED (OR NOT), BUT LEAVE THE STEM INTACT! (BARTLETT OR BOSC PEARS WORK WELL, BUT ANY FIRM PEAR WILL DO THE TRICK)

PREPARATION

1. In a pan large enough to hold the fruit in a single layer, combine all of the ingredients except for the pears and bring to boil, then reduce heat to simmer.

2. Gently place pears into liquid, cover, and "poach" for about 15 minutes, turning pears once along the way so that both sides are evenly covered and cooked. Pears are ready when tender but not mushy and have taken on a beautiful color. Transfer pears to a plate.

3. Boil the remaining liquid, uncovered, until it is reduced by at least half. In fact, keep your eye on it and reduce it until it reaches a thick consistency that you like. I cook it down until it becomes almost a glaze.

4. Now pour it over the pears and serve it as is. Or top it off with ice cream. Or whipped cream. Or top the ice cream with the syrup. Oh, you get the idea.

HOMEMADE WHIPPED CREAM

Cool Whip is cool. Reddi-wip is ready. But it's a piece of cake to whip up your own that's superior to either of those. All you need is some form of blender. Or fast hands.

Coldness matters, so even though you could beat the cream in a glass bowl, it works very in a chilled stainless steel one, which should be put into the freezer about 15 minutes beforehand.

ABOUT 2 CUPS

INGREDIENTS
1 CUP HEAVY CREAM, VERY COLD
1–2 TABLESPOONS SUGAR (EITHER GRANULATED OR CONFECTIONERS' WILL DO)
1 TEASPOON VANILLA EXTRACT

PREPARATION
Place all ingredients into cold bowl and whisk on high speed using electric beaters or immersion blender until medium "peaks" form, about 1 minute. (You can also whisk by hand, which will take you a couple of minutes more.) So whip it good. But know that if you whip it too much, you could end up with something more like butter.

Note on "peaks": You'll notice a change in the texture of the cream as you whip it. It thickens in stages called "peaks." First, trails start to build up and overlap each other. Those are soft peaks. Next, medium peaks form, which is what most of us think of as whipped cream . . . just the kind you'd want to put atop any dessert that warrants it, or directly into your own pie hole. As much as the notion of "stiff peaks" might be attractive to some, the thickness and volume of the cream at this stage is generally reserved for spreading on cakes or for recipes that call for "folding" in cream.

CHOCOLATE-COVERED STRAWBERRIES

Two ingredients to glory. Chocolate. Strawberries. That is all. Melt and dip. Now, I must tell you that there is a "right" temperature at which chocolate is called "tempered," which means that it will be real smooth and shiny when it "sets." But you should know that tempering is a pain in the butt and I don't have the time, patience, or interest in doing it . . . IF I can just simply melt and dip without having to worry about it. That is the case here if you (like me) are totally fine to give up some beauteous perfection in exchange for getting it done quickly and quite well.

P.S. No one has ever refused my chocolate-covered strawberries because they weren't as pretty as the five-buck version at Godiva.

Note: You MUST make sure that the berries are COMPLETELY dry before you dip them. Otherwise you're making a mess. I have actually used a hair blower to dry mine. Seriously.

INGREDIENTS

12 OUNCES QUALITY CHOCOLATE (I FIND 60–70 PERCENT CACAO IS BEST, BUT USE OTHER CHOCOLATE IF YOU MUST)

1 PINT/POUND FRESH STRAWBERRIES

PREPARATION

1. Clean and dry!!! the strawberries.

2. Chop the chocolate into small chunks. Place it into a heatproof/microwave-safe bowl.

3. Melt the chocolate by either A) boiling a few inches of water in a medium-size saucepan and setting the bowl of chocolate over it to melt, stirring until smooth; or B) melting the chocolate in a microwave, in 30-second intervals, stirring in between until fully melted.

4. Line a sheet pan with parchment paper. Dip the berries into the chocolate, holding them by the stem, and set them onto the parchment paper. Refrigerate until firm. Enjoy.

CHOCOLATE TRUFFLES

Once again, allow me to present you with an incredibly lush and luscious dessert that looks impressive and complicated to make . . . but isn't. The chocolate truffle. Learned to make it in cooking school and was surprised to find that it's basically two ingredients: chocolate and heavy cream. So, get yourself some good quality chocolate—brands like Callebaut, Valrhona, and Scharffen Berger among others are very good, but you could also try packaged semisweet chocolate chips—and you will soon be serving your friends and family something fantastic. (And saving a buttload of money.)

Note: Just so you know, these little chocolate delicacies look a whole lot prettier and more professional when they're dusted with either cocoa powder or confectioners' sugar, or rolled in crushed nuts. So dust 'em! Shredded coconut wouldn't be too bad, either.

MAKES ABOUT TWO DOZEN TRUFFLES

INGREDIENTS
1 CUP HEAVY CREAM
8 OUNCES GOOD-QUALITY BITTERSWEET
    CHOCOLATE, CHOPPED
CONFECTIONERS' SUGAR OR UNSWEETENED COCOA
    POWDER, AS NEEDED

PREPARATION

1. Heat the cream in a pot until it's steaming hot; it doesn't have to reach a boil. Put the chocolate pieces in a bowl, pour hot cream on top, and stir until chocolate is melted and everything melds together into one cohesive whole. FYI: Congrats, you've made "ganache."

2. Chill about an hour or two until solid. Now you're going to scoop out about a tablespoon of the ganache at a time and quickly roll it into a ball. You might want to use a melon baller for that job, or even gloves, to minimize melting and sticking to your hands. Line up all your finished balls on a baking sheet lined with parchment or wax paper. You're almost there . . .

3. If they become soft, put them back in the refrigerator or even freezer for a few minutes. Then, roll them in cocoa powder, confectioners' sugar, or perhaps finely ground nuts.

4. Serve with pride, or wrap them well and they'll be good in the fridge for the next few days . . . if they're not inhaled by then.

NOTHING TOPS NUTELLA TOPPING

I've long maintained that Nutella is the crack cocaine of the kitchen. With the texture of creamy peanut butter and the tastes of chocolate and hazelnut, the stuff is amazing and addictive. You can spread it on whatever you want, but I'm fine scooping it right from the jar into my mouth. However, if you want to turn it into an awesome sauce that is literally "over the top" (to *pour* over ice cream or pound cake, for example, or directly into your mouth), here you go. You're welcome.

NUMBER OF SERVINGS DEPENDS ON HOW MANY OTHERS YOU'RE WILLING TO SHARE WITH.

INGREDIENTS
1 CUP NUTELLA (OR OTHER CHOCOLATE HAZELNUT SPREAD)
1 PINT HEAVY CREAM

PREPARATION

1. Place Nutella and cream in saucepan over low heat and whisk together until well blended.

2. Pour it on stuff. Rejoice.

LEMON-GLAZED CUPCAKES

This one is all about the glaze. The icing. Effortless. Elegant. Excellent. So much so, that in the interest of full disclosure, I'll use packaged, store-bought mix for the cupcakes. If you feel like making your own cupcake mix from scratch, go for it. But if you find a decent mix (I've used Arrowhead Mills Organic Vanilla Cake Mix) for the cupcakes, or a regular cake for that matter, you will still be a winner in my eyes . . . because your icing is so damn good!

INGREDIENTS

6 CUPCAKES, MADE FROM A BOX, OR FROM SCRATCH
    BECAUSE YOU'RE AMBITIOUS

Icing
2 TABLESPOONS LEMON JUICE
1½ CUPS CONFECTIONERS' SUGAR

PREPARATION

1. In a small bowl, stir lemon juice and confectioners' sugar until smooth.

2. Pour over cupcakes.

3. Let set 30 minutes, if you can resist that long.

BIG-TIME BISCOTTI (SOMEWHAT INTUITIVE)

I'll admit it, I'm a simpleton. At least when it comes to dessert. Gimme a solid, crunchy cookie and I'm happy. There are four steps to this one (two more than I usually prefer), but they're uncomplicated and even kind of fun to make. More importantly, they're fantastic. Feeling ambitious? Dip 'em in melted chocolate or top 'em off with a drizzle of that lemon glaze (page 223). Hello!

MAKES ABOUT 2 DOZEN

INGREDIENTS

1 CUP SUGAR (AND A LITTLE MORE FOR
    SPRINKLING)
1 STICK UNSALTED BUTTER, MELTED
1½ TEASPOON VANILLA EXTRACT
1½ TEASPOON ALMOND EXTRACT
1 CUP ALMONDS, LIGHTLY TOASTED AND COARSELY
    CHOPPED
3 EGGS
2¾ CUP FLOUR
1½ TEASPOON BAKING POWDER
¼ TEASPOON SALT
¼ CUP DRIED FRUIT, SUCH AS CHERRIES,
    CRANBERRIES, RAISINS

PREPARATION

1. Preheat oven to 350°F. Line a baking sheet with parchment paper.

2. Mix sugar, butter, and extracts in a large bowl. Blend in almonds and eggs. Add in flour, baking powder, salt, and dried fruit, and mix until everything blends together. Form a ball of dough and refrigerate it for half an hour.

3. Cut the dough in half and form two separate rectangular-shaped "logs" that are about 2½ inches wide. Place them on a baking sheet and in the oven for about 30 minutes, until lightly golden. Transfer carefully to a rack to cool.

4. Using a sharp (serrated is ideal) knife, slice into individual pieces, each about an inch wide. Carefully place the pieces on a baking sheet and back into the oven for another 20 minutes or so until they turn golden brown. Remove and cool them again on a rack. Sprinkle them with sugar. Save some for me. Please.

CINNAMON SAUTÉED BANANAS

Inspired by Julia Child, this brings out the best in a banana, which can be topped with anything from ice cream to whipped cream to heavy cream.

MAKES 4 SERVINGS

INGREDIENTS
2–3 TABLESPOONS UNSALTED BUTTER
4 LARGE, FIRMLY RIPE BANANAS
2 TABLESPOONS SUGAR
1 TEASPOON CINNAMON
1 TABLESPOON FRESH LEMON JUICE

PREPARATION

1. Peel the bananas; cut in half lengthwise.

2. In a nonstick frying pan over medium high heat add butter until sizzling. Add bananas and top with sugar, cinnamon, and lemon juice. Sauté until caramelized and tender, about 3–4 minutes.

3. Serve with ice cream, sour cream, or heavy cream.

WATERMELON RASPBERRY SORBET

Almost every recipe you see for sorbet uses sugar. Not mine. No water, either. Only fruit. It's good. And it's sweet . . . if the fruit is sweet. So get sweet fruit. The acidity from the citrus accentuates the sweet factor. Or add a little sugar, agave syrup, or honey if you think it needs it.

SERVES 4

INGREDIENTS
2 CUPS SEEDLESS WATERMELON
1 CUP FRESH RASPBERRIES
1 TABLESPOON FRESH LEMON OR LIME JUICE

PREPARATION

1. In a blender, puree watermelon, berries, and lemon juice until smooth. (You could strain it as this point; I don't.)

2. If you have an ice cream maker, do whatever it tells you to do at this point. If not, transfer the sorbet to a plastic container and freeze until firm. Obviously it can be made well ahead of time and kept frozen.

3. When ready to serve, defrost about 30 minutes or more ahead of time. Garnish with fresh raspberries. (Or a shot of liqueur for the adults.)

BLUEBERRY CRUMBLE

Making a fruit pie usually takes some patience, entails a level of know-how, and requires a little skill. My blueberry crumble eliminates those annoying barriers. It's scrumptious and luxurious, yet not overly sweet. Uncomplicated and wanting for nothing more than a scoop of ice cream or a blast of whipped cream.

INGREDIENTS

For filling
2 PINTS FRESH BLUEBERRIES
2 TABLESPOONS FRESH LEMON JUICE
1 TEASPOON LEMON ZEST
¼ TEASPOON VANILLA
¼ CUP SUGAR
1 TABLESPOON CORNSTARCH
¼ TEASPOON CINNAMON

For topping
1 CUP ALL-PURPOSE FLOUR
¼ CUP GRANULATED SUGAR
¼ CUP BROWN SUGAR
6 TABLESPOONS COLD, UNSALTED BUTTER, DICED
½ CUP QUICK-COOKING OATS
½ CUP SLICED ALMONDS
⅛ TEASPOON SALT

PREPARATION

1. Preheat oven to 350°F.

2. In one bowl, mix blueberries with lemon juice, zest, and vanilla. In another bowl, whisk sugar, cornstarch, and cinnamon. Toss dry mixture with blueberries until evenly coated. Pour into an 8- or 9-inch square baking dish.

3. I like assembling the topping by hand, but you could also pulse a processor or another type of mixer. Mix flour, sugars, and butter until it's coarse and crumbly, then add the oatmeal, almonds, and salt and stir until all combined.

4. Spread the topping evenly over the fruit and bake for about 40 minutes, until berries are bubbling and topping is golden brown. Let it cool a bit, if you can wait, and serve it with whipped cream, ice cream, or straight up.

SERIOUS CHOCOLATE CAKE

It's truly astounding to behold what creation is possible using only chocolate, butter, and eggs. In this case, it is an intense, dense, and decadent cake made without flour or added sugar. (So if you have any chocolate-loving, gluten-free friends and family, they'll surely appreciate this.) Not quite as easy as it may sound, but well worth the attempt when you're ready. Ready? Okay, let me walk you through this one step by step. . . .

Note: By the way, you're going to want to use what's called a "springform" pan for this one, ideally a 10-inch, because they spring open, which allows for an easy release of the dense cake.

8 SERVINGS, MAYBE MORE

INGREDIENTS
1 POUND BEST-QUALITY CHOCOLATE (60–70 PERCENT CACAO), CHOPPED INTO SMALLISH CHUNKS
2 STICKS UNSALTED BUTTER PLUS ABOUT 2 TABLESPOONS MORE FOR "GREASING"
6 EGGS

PREPARATION

1. While you preheat your oven to 425°F, also bring a few inches of water to a simmer in a medium saucepan. Grab some of that "extra" butter and "grease" your new springform pan (meaning to spread the soft butter around the pan with your fingers or a paper towel or, ideally, with the very wrapping paper that the butter comes in). Now line that pan with parchment paper. So far, so good.

2. Melt the chocolate and two sticks of butter in a metal or glass heatproof bowl over your simmering water. Turn off the water when all melted, but you can let it rest there warmly for the next few minutes.

3. Believe it or not, we need another bowl, and more simmering water. The eggs go into a bowl, the bowl goes over the simmering water, and you whisk them until they begin to thicken (maybe 3–5 minutes). At that point, take them off the heat, but continue to beat them for another five minutes. Really.

4. Time to blend the eggs with the melted chocolate butter. Put half of the egg mixture into the chocolate and don't whip it, but more gently "fold" it in, yet still incorporating

Short Order Dad

232

thoroughly. (A soft, rubber spatula is good for this, by the way.) Now fold in the other half of the eggs. Doing great.

5. Pour that beauteous batter evenly into your pan and cover it with a piece of aluminum foil that you will have buttered so that it won't stick to the batter.

6. One last key step: using probably all of that water you have had simmering, and then some, you are going to create a bath for your cake pan. So put the cake pan into a baking dish (or roasting pan) with high sides and fill it with enough hot water *to come halfway up the cake pan.* Seriously. (Incidentally, you have just made an official "bain-marie.")

7. Bake for five minutes, then remove the foil and continue baking for 10 minutes longer. By that point, you should see that it "sets," meaning "to firm" in the pan. When it does, take it out of the hot water bath and let it sit until it cools completely. Then you can spring it open . . . slice it . . . top it off with a dollop of fresh whipped cream . . . and marvel at your bad self.

AFFOGATO

I was taken by how great this was the very first time I had it . . . and how surprisingly simple. Just hot espresso poured over vanilla ice cream. (*Affogato* means *drowned* in Italian.) The result is cold, creamy, bittersweet, and delectable. Although you could leave it at that, I'm big on "gilding the lily." In this case, that means adding a little something something over the top. I like toffee, so I crunch up a bit of Heath bar or Skor and scatter it on. (Or try Biggie's Crack Toffee if you can.) You could also shave chocolate on, or top it with chopped (candied, page 81) nuts. As they say, it's all good.

FOR 1

INGREDIENTS
1 SHOT ESPRESSO
1 SERVING VANILLA ICE CREAM

PREPARATION

1. Pour one over the other.

2. Gild the lily.

3. Smile and say *grazie*.

OLD-FASHIONED NEW YORK EGG CREAM

(Hint: there is no egg in it.)
Think of it as the soda in the ice cream soda. In Brooklyn, they call it an egg cream. It's awesome.

FOR 1

INGREDIENTS
1 LARGE TABLESPOON CHOCOLATE SYRUP (FOX'S
   U-BET IS THE GOLD STANDARD)
2 OUNCES WHOLE MILK
6 OUNCES SELTZER

PREPARATION

1. Pour the chocolate syrup in your glass first, then the milk.

2. Start streaming in the seltzer and stirring simultaneously.

3. Try not to let it overflow onto the counter. Although that means you've achieved the right level of fizz, it also means you've wasted some nectar of the gods.

Note: The default flavor for traditional egg creams is chocolate. However, you can readily substitute with vanilla syrup instead if that's your thing.

Photo by Robert Rosenthal

COCKTAILS (WHEEL GREASERS)

For Adults Only.

I wonder whether the admonition to "drink responsibly" is an oxymoron. Let's face it: don't we already have enough responsibility in our lives? Job. Customers. Kids. Decisions. Paying bills. Making deadlines. Watching your weight. Mowing the lawn. Filling the tank. Initiating foreplay. Then there's moral responsibility, civic responsibility, and fiduciary responsibility. Aren't there times when you just want to say to hell with responsibility? Well, those times often call for a drink.

Yet you can't even do that without being constantly reminded by every single ad for beer, wine, or booze to "drink responsibly." Well, I've got news—the last thing I want to be when I'm drinking . . . is responsible. All this responsibility is half the reason for drinking in the first place.

I'm not advocating inebriation. Or irresponsibility. I'm merely suggesting that even perfectly law-abiding and otherwise responsible grownups have every right to enjoy the occasional adult beverage without guilt. (Just NEVER drive.) So if you're bothered by assorted ills, angsts, nagging negativity, or you're just in the mood for a good old cocktail, here are five you should know how to make.

THE MARTINI

Married with children, you're looking for a little levity with a soigné facade. To be enjoyed with company or solo, the martini is a sophisticated cocktail. There is something genuinely cool about it too—the ritual, the shape of the glass, the purity of the liquid, interrupted only by glorious green olives. A drink for adults, its whole gestalt says, "this is not for kids, I'm a big boy now."

The original, classic version is made with British gin, just an eyedrop or two of dry vermouth, straight up, ice cold, olives and a twist, (so you can eat while you drink). Make it vodka if you must, but know that any 'tini made with watermelon, kiwi, chocolate, or anything other than gin or vodka is not a martini, it's a high-octane, Technicolor dessert. For purists like me, gin is the choice. And one is enough as there's something about that spirit's almost hallucinogenic effectiveness that makes everything else seem like mother's milk. Remember, there's a fine line between dirty martinis and nasty divorce. Speaking of which, if I want dirt in my food, I'll eat it directly from the ground. Dirty is for sex, not martinis.

> "I like to have a martini,
> Two at the very most.
> After three I'm under the table,
> After four I'm under my host."
> —Dorothy Parker

Oh, one more thing: there is a version of the martini known as a Vesper martini that I adore. Rather than choosing between gin and vodka, the Vesper uses both. And rather than vermouth, it calls for Lillet Blanc, a perfectly fruity and fragrant aperitif that makes this cocktail the favorite of James Bond. And me.

CLASSIC MARTINI

INGREDIENTS
ICE
½ OUNCE (MORE *OR LESS*) DRY VERMOUTH,
    PREFERABLY NOILLY PRAT
2½ OUNCES LONDON DRY GIN, SUCH AS BEEFEATER,
    OR VODKA
LEMON TWIST, FOR GARNISH
GREEN OLIVE (OPTIONAL)

PREPARATION

1. Fill a cocktail shaker with ice and pour in the dry vermouth (which, as noted, you can pour out at this point if you want it dry).

2. Add gin or vodka, stir briskly, and strain into chilled cocktail glass.

3. Garnish with lemon and/or olive.

Note: For a "dirty martini," just add a splash of brine from the olive jar.

But remember . . . Dirty is for sex, not martinis.

THE VESPER MARTINI

INGREDIENTS

3 OUNCES LONDON DRY GIN
1 OUNCE VODKA
½ OUNCE LILLET BLANC
LEMON PEEL FOR GARNISH

PREPARATION

1. Add all the ingredients to a cocktail shaker or mixing glass filled with ice.

2. Stir, and strain into a chilled cocktail glass.

3. Rub a slice of lemon peel along the rim of the glass and drop it in.

MARGARITA

Everything is getting on your nerves. Your boss. Traffic. The nightly news. Taxes. You might consider tequila.

Tequila can be calming or corrupting, depending on how you want to play it. You can sip a smoky Don Julio Reposado to calm your nerves, soothe your stomach, and awaken your sense of adventure. At least that's how it starts. How it ends depends on your appetite for adventure. Too much tequila invariably leads to enthusiastic, wild-eyed mischief, followed by outrageous behavior, and then, generally, a misdemeanor.

There always seems to be an element of danger associated with tequila. I suspect that often derives from that first college trip to Cancún, when you go to some place with a name like Carlos 'n Charlie's, where the waiters come along to your table with a type of elongated flask-like device, and inject a dose or two of cheap tequila down your gullet, returning repeatedly, until, perhaps, you find yourself semiconscious, with your pants around your ankles, in a Mexican whorehouse, yelling for your mama.

Jokes aside, you already know how good a margarita is. It has that classic combo of sweet and sour that supports (and perhaps masks) the taste of tequila. Although generally made with an orange liqueur, one of the best I ever had was at an authentic Mexican restaurant in Southern California. So I asked the bartender for the recipe. Lo and behold—no orange liqueur. She used agave instead, and her tequila of choice was Chinaco Blanco. Viva Mexico!

INGREDIENTS

COARSE SALT AND CUT LIME, IF RIMMING GLASS

1½–2 OUNCES TEQUILA (BLANCO OR SILVER, 100 PERCENT AGAVE)

1 OUNCE FRESHLY SQUEEZED LIME JUICE

1 OUNCE AGAVE SYRUP (OR COINTREAU)

LIME WEDGES FOR GARNISH

PREPARATION

1. If rimming the glass with salt, just run a piece of cut lime around the perimeter of the glass and dip it in a plate of salt.

2. Vigorously shake the tequila, lime juice, and agave syrup together with cracked ice in a cocktail shaker for a half a minute, until thoroughly chilled.

3. Either pour directly into a boring old rocks glass OR strain it and serve "straight up" in a fabulous margarita or martini-type glass. Olé!

Cocktails (Wheel Greasers)

241

CAIPIRINHA

For all you do, you're feeling a little unappreciated, even unloved. Say hello to the Caipirinha. From over fifty trips to Brazil, three things stand out in my mind: grilled hearts of palm, sultry women, and caipirinhas, the potently sexy national cocktail. Made of only lime, sugar, and cachaça, the spirit distilled from sugarcane, capirinha literally translates into "little hillbilly." But think of it as liquid love. So be careful, for the first sip may surprise you, yet as you continue to stir the lime sugar syrup you'll soon discover that these things go down like a baby's butt on a waterslide.

Saúde!

SERVES 2

INGREDIENTS
1 JUICY LIME, CUT INTO 16 PIECES, WHITE PITH REMOVED
2–3 TABLESPOONS GRANULATED SUGAR
4–6 OUNCES CACHAÇA (OR VODKA)
ICE CUBES

PREPARATION

1. In a rocks glass, use a "muddler" or wooden spoon to mash together half the lime pieces with half the sugar, extracting as much juice as possible to produce a "syrup."

2. Add 2–3 ounces of cachaça and stir well to incorporate all of the ingredients together.

3. Fill with ice and enjoy.

Note: Go ahead and make it with vodka if you don't have cachaça; then you've got yourself a caipiroska instead.

SANGRIA

You're out on a date, and you want to bring her home late, to sin. It could start with sangria. First of all, it's generally consumed by the pitcher. And what a tasty-looking pitcher it is, filled with chilled, purple-colored grape juice and charming chunks of fruit floating about. What you may not know is that it ain't just cheap red wine—it's red wine spiked with brandy or rum or any other flammable intoxicant a bartender needs to move. Then it's polished off with sweet liqueur, such as Grand Marnier, and a splash of carbonation.

So it's fruit punch with a punch, which also makes it ideal for a gathering of adults. You don't need a great bottle of wine; a decent one will do. Variations abound: you can make it red or white, choose from an array of fruits to include, bump up the booze factor, adjust the sweetness as desired, and even bring it some bubbly. The ingredients are basic; how much you use of each is up to you.

8 SERVINGS

INGREDIENTS
ASSORTED FRUIT, CUT INTO SMALL PIECES OR SLICES, ABOUT 1–2 CUPS (APPLE AND CITRUS WITH SKIN ON ARE MOST COMMON, BUT YOU CAN BE CREATIVE AND USE PLUMS, MANGOES, GRAPES, BERRIES, MOST ANYTHING, BUT I'D AVOID BANANAS)

1 BOTTLE OF DRY WINE, RED OR WHITE (E.G., SPANISH RIOJA IS GOOD, AS IS PINOT GRIGIO)

½ CUP BRANDY OR COGNAC (FOR RED SANGRIA) OR VODKA, FRUIT-FLAVORED OR NOT (FOR WHITE)

¼ CUP ORANGE LIQUEUR OR PEACH SCHNAPPS

2–4 TABLESPOONS SUGAR (GRANULATED OR SUPERFINE), OR TO TASTE

SELTZER, CLUB SODA, OR SPRITE FOR TOPPING OFF

ICE CUBES FOR SERVING

PREPARATION

1. Place fruit in a small pitcher; add everything else except for sparkling beverage and ice.

2. Stir well to combine, making sure to dissolve sugar, and chill for as long as overnight.

3. Pour into ice-filled glasses, making sure to include some fruit, and top with a shot of sparkling beverage.

MOJITO

You're looking for a reason to celebrate something. How about the fact that we've now resumed relations with Cuba? Let's make mojitos.

The Cuban classic features the fragrance of mint and the bright flavor of lime, balanced by a bit of sweetness and a touch of fizz. All good, as they say. You'll need to do a little "muddling," the fancy way of saying mashing together the ingredients. Don't have a muddler? Use whatever works, like a fork. As you serve it, mention to your friends you're no longer a bartender; now you'd like to be referred to as a mixologist.

INGREDIENTS

½ LIME, CUT INTO QUARTERS
4–5 SPRIGS OF MINT
1–2 TEASPOONS SUGAR
1–2 OUNCES OF GOOD RUM
SPLASH OF SELTZER OR CLUB SODA

PREPARATION

1. Place limes, mint, and sugar in an 8-ounce cocktail glass and muddle (or mash) until blended and syrupy.

2. Add rum and seltzer; garnish with mint leaves.

3. Enjoy with warm quesadillas (page 91) and mango tomato salsa (page 202). Invite me to that party.

One cannot think well, love well, sleep well, if one has not dined well.

—Virginia Woolf

Keep in Touch!

Twitter and Instagram: @shortorderdad

Facebook: www.facebook.com/ShortOrderDad

Website: shortorderdad.com/

INDEX